Angola

The Hidden History of Washington's War

Ernest Harsch and Tony Thomas

Angola

Angola

The Hidden History of Washington's War

Ernest Harsch and Tony Thomas

Edited with an introduction
by Malik Miah

PATHFINDER PRESS, INC.   NEW YORK

PATHFINDER PRESS, Inc.
410 West Street, New York, N.Y. 10014

Contents

About the Authors   8

Introduction   9

PART I

By Ernest Harsch

The Roots of American Intervention   15

Origins of the Independence Struggle   25

A New Challenge: Portuguese Neocolonialism   49

From Coalition to Civil War   61

The Factional Struggle for Power   77

The CIA's "Operation Angola"   97

South Africa: NATO's Secret Partner   109

The Stakes for South African Imperialism   121

PART II

The American People and the Angolan Freedom Struggle   133

By Tony Thomas

Hands Off Angola!   153

Bibliography   157

MAPS:

Africa   2

Angola—districts   7

Angola—peoples and resources   43

ANGOLA: Districts and district capitals

About the Authors

ERNEST HARSCH, as a staff writer for the international newsweekly *Intercontinental Press,* has written extensively on Angola, South Africa, and African politics during the last two years. He also contributed to the book *Life in Capitalist America: Private Profit and Social Decay* published by Pathfinder Press in 1975.

TONY THOMAS is a central leader of the Socialist Workers Party and a staff writer for the *Militant,* a socialist newsweekly. In January 1976 he launched a national speaking tour on the topic: "Angola: The Next Vietnam?" He edited and was a major contributor to *Black Liberation and Socialism* (Pathfinder, 1974), and has written several pamphlets.

About the Editor

MALIK MIAH coordinates the activities of the Socialist Workers Party in the Black liberation movement and is a member of the party's National Committee. He also has been touring the U.S. as part of the SWP's campaign to end all American intervention into Angolan affairs. He is the author of the pamphlet *The U.S Role in Southern Africa* (Pathfinder, 1973).

Introduction

Angola, 1975: ". . . is not, never has been, and never will be a question of the use of U.S. forces."

> President Gerald Ford
> December 19, 1975

Vietnam, 1962: ". . . no present plans for the commitment of American combat forces. . . . It is their war."

> Assistant Secretary of State
> W. Averell Harriman
> February 13, 1962

American intervention into the affairs of the peoples of Angola has gone on for many years. Washington was a mainstay of Lisbon's war against the Angolan liberation movement, and has backed the intervention of South African armed forces during the Angolan civil war. Ever since the sixteenth century, Angola has been considered a valuable colonial possession because of its rich natural resources and strategic location. Today, the aim of the U.S. rulers remains to keep Angola under imperialist economic domination.

Written as the events in Angola are unfolding, this book documents how, before the April 1974 coup in Portugal, Washington pursued this policy by giving Lisbon military and economic aid—directly and through the North Atlantic Treaty Organization. Many of the guns, planes, and napalm bombs used by the Portuguese to kill African men, women, and children were American-made. In detail it shows how, in the situation that developed after the 1974 Portuguese coup, Washington sought to develop and protect its interests by intervening in the struggle between the three nationalist groups. To date tens of millions of dollars' worth of direct military aid has been given to one side in the civil war. Washington also set out to recruit American and European mercenaries, and secretly encouraged South Africa's incursion into Angola.

In response to this imperialist aggression in Angola, the overwhelming sentiment of the American population has been "No more Vietnams!" The antiwar voice in the United States has been so loud that the capitalist politicians in Congress have felt compelled to vote down the use of any more "covert" funds in Angola. Representative Charles Diggs, a leader of the Congressional Black Caucus, explained the dilemma of the ruling class this way: "The American public, in particular the Black community, will not sit idly by as the administration attempts militarily to involve this country in support of the interests of the white minority regime in South Africa."

Trade unions, church groups, student organizations, and many others have roundly condemned U.S. intervention in Angola. Demonstrations, rallies, picket lines, and other activities have been organized to tell the Washington war-makers to get out.

Blacks in particular have no desire to fight their Angolan brothers and sisters, who are seeking the same goals as Black Americans: freedom, equality, and an end to national oppression. The millions of dollars being used for imperialist purposes in Angola should be building more homes for Blacks and the working poor, providing more jobs for the unemployed, buying more buses and building more schools to end segregation in education.

The deciding factor, in the final analysis, in what the U.S. government is capable of doing in Angola will be the response of the American people. If strong pressure is placed on the war-makers in Washington, their hands can be tied. As the Vietnam protests showed, the organization and mobilization of American and world public opinion can play a decisive role. Such a mass antiwar movement on an international scale is needed to ensure the right of the Angolan peoples to self-determination. "No more Vietnams" and "Hands off Angola" are the demands that can unify and mobilize American antiwar sentiment.

Angola: The Hidden History of Washington's War is the first book to provide a socialist analysis of the civil war and imperialist intervention in Angola. Part I, by Ernest Harsch, details the background of the factional struggle and the social forces involved. He carefully documents the extent and character of U.S., Portuguese, and South African intervention, and analyzes the origin and evolution of each of the major nationalist organizations.

The position taken by revolutionary socialists on the events in Angola is elaborated in Part II. It includes a report given by Tony Thomas to the National Committee of the Socialist Workers Party in January 1976, and a statement adopted by that body.

The SWP statement outlines the type of antiwar campaign that can and must be organized in the United States, and worldwide, to counter Washington's aims in Angola.

Malik Miah
February 1, 1976

Part I

The Roots of
American Intervention

In late 1975, a new name suddenly appeared in front-page newspaper headlines: Angola. Within a matter of weeks, it became more than just the name of a West African country engulfed by civil war. It began to symbolize American imperialism's general offensive against the peoples of Africa, Asia, and Latin America who are struggling for freedom, for an end to foreign domination. "Angola" threatened to enter the special vocabulary of similar words: Santo Domingo, Vietnam, Cambodia, Laos.

The U.S. intervention in Angola came at a time when the memory of Washington's long and brutal war against the Indochinese peoples was still fresh. In fact, the scenario sounded all too much like a rerun of the early 1960s. First came the demagogic warnings about "Soviet expansionism" in Africa and its alleged threat to "American security." Then came the revelations that Washington was already deeply involved, that for months large amounts of U.S. arms and money had been funneled to one of the sides in the civil war, that American pilots were flying reconnaissance planes over Angola, and that the Central Intelligence Agency (CIA) had recruited hundreds of mercenaries for an "undercover army." A logical question that must have entered many minds was: If given a free hand, how far would Washington go? Would U.S. troops be next?

The American intervention in Angola fits in with a pattern established by Washington at the end of the Second World War. The post-war period, the beginning of what Washington euphemistically labeled the "American Century," was marked by the collapse of the old British, French, Belgian, and Dutch empires and by the rapid expansion of American economic and political interests throughout much of the world. The mass upsurge against colonialism that began in Asia in the late 1940s and spread to Africa in the late 1950s and early 1960s forced the major European powers to give up formal political control of their overseas "possessions" and adopt neocolonial methods of rule. The investors and bankers on Wall Street saw themselves as the natural heirs to these former colonies. Through their giant imperialist trusts—and with the full backing of Washington's political and military power—they were well in the forefront of the scramble to exploit the resources of the underdeveloped world.

Portugal's colonial empire lasted longer than the others. But with the growth of national liberation movements in its African colonies of Angola, Mozambique, and Guinea-Bissau in the 1960s, that empire was seriously shaken. The policy makers in Washington feared that the Black African nationalist struggles might escape control if Lisbon was forced to withdraw from Africa precipitously as a result of the political and economic strain of its colonial wars. The White House thus decided, as early as 1961, to prop up the feeble Portuguese empire as long as possible.

In March 1961, a massive uprising against Portuguese colonial rule swept northern Angola. It was initiated by the União das Populações de Angola (UPA—Angolan Peoples' Union), a nationalist group led by Holden Roberto. (In 1962 the UPA became the FNLA [Frente Nacional de Libertação de Angola—Angolan National Liberation Front].) The rebellion was met by a brutal Portuguese counterinsurgency campaign that left tens of thousands of Africans dead and devastated large areas of the north. Although the troops used in those operations were Portuguese, the quartermaster was American.

Washington tacitly allowed the Portuguese dictatorship of António de Oliveira Salazar to use American weapons—supplied through the North Atlantic Treaty Organization (NATO)—in its Angola war. William Minter, in his book *Portuguese Africa and the West*, detailed some of these arms: "Material support, in the form of equipment, is given to the [Portuguese] Army's NATO division, to the Navy, and to the Air Force. The NATO division is equipped with American-supplied M-47 tanks, 105-millimetre and 155-millimetre guns, trucks, jeeps, and other technical machinery and vehicles. . . . In 1961, it was admitted later, equipment from this NATO division was used in Angola" (p. 104). Washington loaned two destroyer escorts to Lisbon's navy in 1953. The loans were extended in 1967; and three additional U.S. destroyer escorts had been given to Portugal by 1969. An official Portuguese military publication reported in 1963 that the planes used against Angolan rebels included American F-84 Thunderjets, PV-2 Harpoon bombers, T-6 trainers equipped for armed reconnaissance flights, and C-54 transports. F-86 Saberjets are also thought to have been used by Lisbon in its African wars (see Minter, pp. 105, 106).

Washington also gave one of its favorite weapons—napalm—to the Salazarist dictatorship. Describing the Portuguese military campaign in northern Angola, John Marcum wrote in *The Angolan Revolution, Vol. 1: The Anatomy of an Explosion (1950-1962)*: "By January 1962 outside observers could watch Portuguese planes bomb and strafe African villages, visit the charred remains of towns like Mbanza M'Pangu and M'Pangala, and copy the data from 750-pound napalm bomb casings from which the Portuguese had not removed the labels marked 'Property U.S. Air Force'" (pp. 229-30).

Between 1953 and 1961, Washington sent more than $301 million in military aid and $27 million in economic assistance to the Lisbon regime. For 1962-68, the figures stood at $39 million in military and $124 in economic aid. This figure apparently did not include the seven Douglas B-26 bombers secretly transported from Tucson, Arizona, to Lisbon between June and September 1965. Although it was transacted as a private commercial deal between Lisbon and a company called Aero Associates, Inc., two of the pilots who ferried the planes to Portugal said they were hired by the CIA.

Hundreds of Portuguese troops received U.S. military training, either in Portugal by the Pentagon's Military Assistance Advisory Group or at bases in the United States. Some received instruction at the U.S. counterinsurgency school at Fort Bragg, North Carolina.

During the early 1960s, Washington was also involved, in a more direct fashion, in Angola's northern neighbor, the former Belgian Congo (now Zaïre). As early as 1960, the CIA planned to assassinate Patrice Lumumba, the Congo's first premier and the most outstanding of the Congolese nationalist leaders. (Lumumba was murdered in January 1961 by agents of the imperialist-backed Katanga secessionist regime.) The CIA, with the aid of South African intelligence, recruited mercenaries to fight against

Lumumba's followers. In 1964, Washington armed Moïse Tshombe, former head of the Katanga regime. It helped him crush the rebel followers of Christophe Gbenya by supplying American pilots to fly Belgian paratroopers into Stanleyville, the rebel stronghold, in November 1964.

Although Washington and its Congolese allies managed to quell the rebellions in that country by the late 1960s, it did not want to face a repetition of the Congo crisis in the Portuguese colonies. Adlai E. Stevenson, U.S. ambassador to the United Nations, expressed this concern in a speech to the UN Security Council in 1961. Minter wrote that "Stevenson emphasized the danger of 'premature independence' such as that in the Congo. The problem there had been, he said, that 'the pressure of nationalism rapidly overtook the preparation of the necessary foundation essential to the peaceful and effective exercise of sovereign self-government.' On the one hand this meant that Portugal should be urged to undertake such preparation; this was the main point of the speech. On the other hand, it implied that as long as such preparations were not undertaken voluntarily by Portugal, it was important that the pressure of nationalism be curbed" (pp. 90-91).

Minter cites a State Department document which was a bit more explicit on this point. "The United States," it said, "recognizes the contribution made in Africa by Portugal and believes that it is important that Portugal continue to contribute to stability in that continent." On May 6, 1963, General Lyman Lemnitzer, the commander of NATO forces in Europe, declared: "Portuguese soldiers, while fighting for the defence of principles, are defending land, raw materials, and bases, which are indispensable not only for the defence of Europe, but for the whole Western world" (as quoted by Minter, p. 107).

As they deepened their penetration of the colonial world, American investors preferred to operate in formally independent ex-colonies; without the restrictions of direct political control exercised from London, Paris, or Brussels, U.S. companies were in a better position to compete with their European rivals and establish American economic dominance over some of the underdeveloped countries of Africa and Asia. Portuguese imperialism, however, was extremely weak economically and was forced to allow other imperialist interests to penetrate its "overseas provinces" even while Lisbon maintained its political control. In

April 1965 Lisbon greatly relaxed its restrictions on foreign investment in its African colonies.

In 1966, Cabinda Gulf Oil, a wholly-owned subsidiary of the U.S. Gulf Oil Company, discovered extensive oil deposits off the coast of Cabinda, a tiny enclave north of Angola proper. By the early 1970s the Cabindan oil fields, over which Gulf had a monopoly concession, were producing about 10 million tons of oil a year, ranking Angola as the fourth largest oil producer in Africa, after Libya, Algeria, and Nigeria. It is estimated that the oil deposits in Cabinda could produce between 100 million and 150 million tons yearly by the turn of the century.

The surface rents, bonuses, taxes, royalties, and concession payments Lisbon received from Gulf's operations were a major source of revenue to finance its colonial wars. A Gulf statement admitted that the company had paid Lisbon $11 million in taxes and royalties in 1969 alone. That figure was almost half the 1970 military budget of the Portuguese administration in Angola. (With the sharp rise in oil prices a few years later, these payments skyrocketed to an estimated $500 million a year.)

Although the Gulf oil interests in Angola are the largest, they are not the only ones. The first oil company to cash in on Angola's petroleum deposits was the Belgian Petrofina (Compagnie Financière Belge des Pétroles), which began production in 1955. In 1957 it turned over a third of its shares to the Portuguese administration in Angola, forming Petrangol (Companhia de Petróleos de Angola). Petrangol owned the country's only existing oil refinery, located in Luanda. A number of other companies explored the area off Angola's coast, including the U.S. companies, Occidental and Exxon, and the French ELF-Total (Essences et Lubrificants de France–Total). Before the outbreak of the Angolan civil war, there were thirty-three wells under exploration or in production near Santo António do Zaire in northern Angola. In November 1974, it was reported that the U.S.-controlled Texaco Petróleo de Angola had made a major oil discovery near Santo António do Zaire. Although Texaco did not confirm how extensive the find was, the reserves were estimated by other sources to be as high as ten times those of Cabinda.

Angola has other valuable resources that the American and other imperialist interests have scrambled to secure. Another major export until the civil war was robusta coffee, much of which was shipped to the United States. The value of coffee exports in 1973 stood at $206 million. With a production of

220,000 tons in 1974, Angola became the second most important coffee grower in Africa and the third largest in the world. Most of the coffee plantations in Angola were owned by three companies, all of which were controlled by the Rallet bank of France. Exports were handled by the South African company Inexcafé. Although only about 2 percent of the country's vast and fertile land area was under active commercial agricultural exploitation, there were other export crops including cotton and sisal.

Diamonds are third on Angola's list of riches. The principal diamond fields, in northeastern Angola, are exploited by the Companhia de Diamantes de Angola (Diamang), which is controlled by De Beers Consolidated Mines Ltd. (a subsidiary of the Anglo-American Corporation of South Africa) together with Belgian, British, and American interests. Before the Portuguese relinquished direct control of Angola, the colonial administration in Luanda required a 50 percent share of the diamond profits. In 1972, Angola produced over 2 million carats, valued at about $110 million.

The iron mines in the Cassinga area of Huila district are owned by the Companhia Mineira do Lobito, which is controlled by the West German Krupp enterprise. Iron ore exports in 1973 stood at 6 million tons, worth about $49 million. Other mineral products from Angola include manganese, phosphates (exploited by the Chromalloy American Corporation), copper, beryl, kaolin, granite, marble, sea salt, asphalt rock, and gypsum. Gold, mica, bituminous slate, coal, sulphur, and silicate have also been discovered. Southwest Angola may have the largest deposits of titanium in the world. Since the country was very little prospected until recently, the imperialist powers have barely tapped Angola's vast resources. Angola is thought to have the greatest economic potential of any African country south of the Sahara, with the exception of South Africa.

Washington decided that the best defense of its interests in Angola was to safeguard the status quo, that is, Lisbon's continued political dominance of the Angolan treasure house. There were some American officials, however, who were more farsighted, who realized that Lisbon's colonial empire was doomed despite massive U.S. aid. George Ball, an undersecretary of state during both the Kennedy and Johnson administrations, wrote in *The Discipline of Power* (1968) that "the real danger, of course, is that after a long war of attrition in which her overseas territories were devastated from one end to the other, Portugal would collapse. And the longer the struggle continued, the more likely that the Soviet Union and perhaps China would try to fish in troubled water. . . . the situation, in its very nature, would not be in the best interest of the United States or its Western European allies, since Angola and Mozambique are extensive and strategically important territories, lying at the heart of Africa" (as quoted by Minter, p. 96).

Following the 1961 uprising in northern Angola, some U.S. policy makers saw the possibility that Lisbon might be forced to abandon its colonies. Washington's policy in Portuguese-controlled Africa, as in other parts of the world, was to hedge its bets. While continuing to throw most of its support behind its imperialist ally in Lisbon, the White House also sought to keep open its options toward the emerging Black nationalist leaders. Citing "four official sources," the *New York Times* revealed in its September 25, 1975, issue that as early as 1962 the CIA began sending arms and funds to Holden Roberto.

John Marks, an associate of the Center for National Security Studies (a nongovernment body) and coauthor of *The CIA and the Cult of Intelligence,* provided additional details of this CIA operation in an article that was printed in the December 16, 1975, *Congressional Record.*

Marks cited a former White House aide as saying that during the administration of President Johnson, Washington's policy toward the Portuguese colonies was "to play all ends against the middle." This meant, according to the aide, giving some military and political support to the Salazar dictatorship, while subsidizing the independence groups to a certain degree.

The CIA, the official said, had the "habit of picking out single individuals and making them our guys, somehow assuming they would turn out all right. It was mainly a cash-in-the-envelope kind of thing—conscience money to show American good intentions."

In Angola, the CIA expressed its "good intentions" to Roberto. In Mozambique, according to the official, it was to Dr. Eduardo Mondlane, the principal leader of Frelimo (Frente de Libertação de Moçambique—Mozambique Liberation Front) until his assassination by parcel bomb in early 1969.

Although other nationalist groups existed in Angola and Mozambique, it appears that the White House chose the FNLA and Frelimo as recipients of CIA aid because they were the largest and most active, and therefore the most useful targets for the American attempts to gain future political influence. The FNLA carried out the bulk of the fighting in Angola throughout the early 1960s, as did Frelimo in Mozambique from the mid-1960s until Lisbon agreed in 1974 to grant the colony its independence.

Although Marks's source did not reveal how much aid the CIA had sent to the FNLA and Frelimo, he did note that it was not enough to turn the tide against Lisbon. Until the April 25, 1974, Portuguese coup, the White House continued to place most of its bets on the Salazarist dictatorship. According to the official quoted by Marks, President Nixon halted the CIA's "program aid" to the African independence groups in 1969 as part of an overall policy of easing the pressures against the white regimes in southern Africa. The CIA, however, did not want to close the door on Roberto entirely, and kept him on a $10,000 a year "retainer."

A secret study carried out in 1969 by the National Security Council under the direction of Henry Kissinger, then national security adviser, examined U.S. interests in the region and proposed several policy options to be followed to protect those interests. One of the dangers stressed in the Kissinger study, which was called National Security Study Memorandum 39, was that "the prospect of increasing violence in the area growing out of black insurgency and white reprisal could jeopardize our interests in the future." Some of the U.S. interests cited in the study included American investments in the region and South Africa's strategic location on the Cape of Good Hope, around which much of the world's traded goods are shipped.

Some of Washington's objectives, according to the study, were "to minimize the likelihood of escalation of violence in the area and risk of U.S. involvement," and "to protect economic, scientific and strategic interests and opportunities in the region, including the orderly marketing of South Africa's gold production."

In February 1970, President Nixon officially adopted a new policy toward southern Africa that "tilted" more in the direction of the white minority regimes and that marked a significant increase in Washington's support to Portuguese colonialism. This policy shift was recommended by Kissinger. Nicknamed "Tar Baby" by White House aides, the policy was based on the premise that "the whites are here to stay and the only way constructive change can come about is through them. There is no hope for the blacks to gain the political rights they seek through violence, which will only lead to chaos and increased opportunities for the communists." The general posture of Tar Baby was to "maintain public opposition to racial repression but relax political isolation and economic restrictions on the white states." In addition to adopting various measures that "relaxed" relations with the racist regimes in South Africa and Rhodesia (Zimbabwe), Tar Baby proposed that Washington "continue arms embargo on Portuguese territories, but give more liberal treatment to exports of dual purpose equipment" and "encourage trade and investment in Portuguese territories; full EXIM Bank facilities" (*Kissinger Study*, p. 68).

Since Washington was already breaking the UN's formal arms embargo on the Portuguese colonies, the call for more exports of "dual purpose equipment" that could be used for both civilian and military tasks marked an escalation of the U.S. military support for Lisbon. Minter wrote:

> Increased American support for Portuguese colonialism is reflected in the Nixon administration's decision to allow the sale of two Boeing 707s to Portugal for use in troop transport. Although planes sold to the Portuguese airline (TAP) have in the past served the same purpose, this new sale is distinctive in that the planes are explicitly for troop transport. Still in the old style of deception are the quadrupled exports of herbicides to Portugal in 1970, with a denial that they are being used in Africa; and sales of five Bell helicopters to the Zambezi Development Office in Mozambique, for ostensibly civilian use only. In November 1970, six Portuguese army lieutenants, having deserted from the Portuguese army, testified that they had been trained in West Germany by US guerrilla warfare experts, before being sent to Mozambique. In March 1971, American officers participated in a special training course in Lisbon for Portuguese officers. (p. 154.)

From 1969 to 1972, about $108 million worth of American aircraft and helicopters was exported to Portugal, Mozambique, and Angola. This figure was more than twice that for the period from 1965 to 1968. A number of Rockwell photo-reconnaissance aircraft were sold to Lisbon between 1971 and 1972. In December 1971, Washington authorized a $436 million Export-Import Bank credit loan to Portugal in exchange for continued use of the U.S. military base in the Azores islands. This loan was four times the total amount the Export-Import Bank had extended to Portugal between 1946 and 1971.

By placing virtually all its bets on Lisbon, Washington committed itself to the preservation of Portuguese colonialism in Angola, Mozambique, and Guinea-Bissau. On April 25, 1974, it lost its gamble with the downfall of the Salazarist dictatorship in Lisbon, which opened the way for the granting of formal independence to Portugal's African colonies. If the three major Angolan nationalist organizations had adopted a united approach against continued imperialist maneuvers and intervention, the ability of the White House to influence the course of the "decolonization" process in Angola could have been greatly hampered. The outbreak of the civil war in 1975, however, gave the U.S. imperialists a better opening.

Origins of the
Independence Struggle

The rivalries between the three main Angolan nationalist groups go back many years and are rooted in the evolution of the various Black nationalist currents that developed among the different peoples of Angola. The three main groups are the FNLA (Frente Nacional de Libertação de Angola—Angolan National Liberation Front); the MPLA (Movimento Popular de Libertação de Angola—People's Movement for the Liberation of Angola); and the UNITA (União Nacional para Independência Total de Angola—National Union for the Total Independence of Angola). While each claims to represent the interests of all Angolans, in fact they each remain limited to the ethnic bases from which they emerged.

These cleavages within the Angolan nationalist struggle are but a reflection of Angolan society itself. Before the arrival of the Portuguese, the area now known as Angola was dotted with various kingdoms and tribal groupings that spoke different languages and had different cultures and histories. The Portuguese colonialists seized parts of this region in the late fifteenth century and gradually extended their control. They marked off the borders with no regard for the peoples of the area, in some cases arbitrarily drawing the boundaries through the middle of population centers. This imperialist carving up of Africa was formalized by the European powers at the 1885 Berlin Conference.

The Bakongo living in northern Angola number between one and one and a half million, or about 25 percent of Angola's population. Descended from the ancient Kongo kingdom, which was conquered and destroyed by the Portuguese, French, and

Belgians, the Bakongo now live in the Republic of the Congo, Zaïre, and northern Angola, often migrating across the borders. The Mbundu, also about 25 percent of the population, live in an area of north-central Angola stretching from Luanda on the coast eastward to Malange. The Ovimbundu people, living in the central plateau region, are the largest ethnic group, numbering more than two million and comprising about a third of the population. Other peoples included the Lundas and Chokwes of eastern and northeastern Angola, some of whom spill over the border into Zaïre, the Hereros and Ovambos (Cuanhamas) of southern Angola, who also live in neighboring Namibia (South-West Africa), and the Nyaneka-Humbe, Luvale, Luchazi, Mbunda, Nhengo, and Bushmen scattered throughout eastern and southern Angola.

Nationalist Stirrings

The MPLA arose out of the nationalist currents that developed among the small layer of intellectuals, both African and *mestiço* (of mixed African and Portuguese parenthood), after World War II, principally in the capital of Luanda. Viriato da Cruz and Mário Pintó de Andrade, two of the principal founders of the MPLA, were associated with the nationalist literary journal *Mensagem—A voz dos naturais de Angola,* published in Luanda in the early 1950s. Agostinho Neto, today the MPLA's central leader, was, like Cruz and Andrade, a prominent poet in that period.

These currents were also influenced by the Portuguese Communist Party. According to René Pélissier, in his contribution to the book *Angola,* the PCP appears to have worked with the Liga Nacional Africana (LNA—African National League) and other nationalist groups and recruited a few members and sympathizers during the 1950s. According to an article written by Andrade in 1960, the Partido Comunista de Angola (PCA—Angolan Communist Party), formed in October 1955, joined a nationalist front called the Partido da Luta dos Africanos de Angola (PLUA—Angolan African Struggle Party) in early 1956. PLUA and several other small groups merged in December 1956 to form the MPLA. Andrade later revised the history of the origins of the MPLA, dropping all mention of the PCA (Marcum, pp. 27-29).

The MPLA's program, published in the March 1961 *Portuguese and Colonial Bulletin,* included a series of democratic demands. James Duffy wrote in *Portugal in Africa:* "The programme proposed equal rights for women, a voting age of eighteen years, the abolition of foreign military bases, the end of the forced-labor régime, a minimum wage, and an eight-hour day. Economically, the party required the distribution of estate lands to African farmers, the abolition of the single-crop system, and the transformation of Angola into a modern industrialized country" (pp. 219-20). About the same time, Andrade published a booklet containing the MPLA's "maximum and minimum" programs. According to Marcum, the MPLA's "maximum" program included a pledge to protect private enterprise and "foreign economic activities which were useful" to the country (p. 203).

In the later 1950s the repression by the Portuguese security police forced Cruz, the secretary-general of the MPLA, to flee abroad. The MPLA was a small propaganda group at that time; its strength within Angola was limited to a few clandestine cells. The MPLA, moreover, was only one of nearly a dozen similar groups in Luanda. It did not become a major force within the nationalist movement until several years later when it managed to establish a base among the Mbundu people.

The FNLA was built on the Bakongo nationalist movement in northern Angola that developed in the 1950s. The Bakongo had a long history of resistance to the Portuguese (as did the Mbundu and Ovimbundu), confronting the Portuguese invaders with sporadic wars and uprisings throughout the last half of the nineteenth century. In 1913-14 the Bakongos rose up in an attempt to oust the Portuguese-appointed Kongo king and end forced labor on the white-owned plantations.

Conditions similar to those that led to the 1913-14 uprising were still present in the 1950s and influenced the rise of the modern nationalist movement in the Bakongo areas. In December 1955, there were public protests against forced labor. Three months later, the Portuguese launched a wave of arrests and deportations.

A major factor in heightening the nationalist sentiment among the Bakongo was the anticolonial struggle that was beginning to sweep the rest of Africa. Ghana won its formal independence in 1957. In 1960 the Bakongo in the French and Belgian colonies north of Angola also gained an end to direct colonial rule. This inspired the Bakongo and other peoples in Angola; and in 1959, after elections had been promised in the Belgian-ruled Congo, demonstrations against Portuguese rule were staged in Angola.

It was against this background that the União das Populações do Norte de Angola (UPNA—North Angola Peoples' Union) became the UPA in 1958. The UPNA had backed a Protestant candidate for king of the Kongo in opposition to the Portuguese efforts to appoint a subservient Catholic figurehead. The newly formed UPA, under the leadership of Holden Roberto, gave up any efforts to restore the Kongo monarchy. It formally adopted a pan-Angolan nationalist perspective and called for the independence of Angola (the UPNA had called, instead, for the restoration of the old Kongo kingdom and the separation of the Bakongo areas from the rest of Angola.

The UPA's base was primarily among the Bakongo peasants and plantation workers of northern Angola and those Bakongo workers who had migrated to the Belgian-ruled Congo in search of jobs and to escape the forced labor conditions imposed by the Portuguese. However, as the strongest nationalist current in Angola at the time, the UPA also had some influence in Luanda, in the Dembos area, and among the Mbundu in the cotton-growing region around Malange. The UPA also established contacts with Ovimbundu and Chokwe groups in central and eastern Angola.

The aid the UPA received from Congolese nationalist leaders was an important factor in the UPA's rapid growth. According to Marcum (p. 65), Holden Roberto had known Patrice Lumumba personally since the 1940s. After the Congo gained its independence from Belgium in 1960, Lumumba invited the UPA to set up its headquarters in Léopoldville (later renamed Kinshasa); he helped the UPA spread its influence in Angola by authorizing a series of weekly UPA broadcasts over Radio Léopoldville (p. 86). Roberto also had close ties with Frantz Fanon, the well-known anticolonialist intellectual who was closely identified with the Algerian nationalist struggle. Fanon appears to have had an important influence on the UPA's early actions against the Portuguese.

The nationalist program outlined in the 1960 Declaration of the Steering Committee of the UPA was essentially similar to that of the MPLA, although more general. "Angola," it said, "would form an autonomous state, establish its own democratic responsible government, conforming to the traditions and needs of the land—a government fully competent to direct public affairs, organize public services, national economy, education, public health, in the best interests of all its citizens and excluding all foreign interference" (as quoted by Duffy, p. 218).

The nationalist currents in the Ovimbundu areas did not gain significant strength until the mid-1960s, although a number of small groups emerged earlier. One of the groups, the clandestine Juventude Cristã de Angola (JCA—Christian Youth of Angola), composed of Ovimbundu living in Luanda, contacted the UPA in early 1961 and asked to join Roberto's organization. Another Ovimbundu nationalist current was formed by Julio Chinovola Cacunda, who carried out political agitation among the African troops serving in the Portuguese army and organized a series of clandestine cells in Nova Lisboa, Lobito, Luanda, Sá da Bandeira, and other towns (see Marcum, pp. 106-8, 111). Both of these groups, as well as other Ovimbundu organizations, were destroyed by the Portuguese in 1961.

Another social force that influenced the early Black nationalist movements was the small but significant Angolan working class. Its impact was to be felt again more than a decade later, in a more direct fashion, after the Portuguese coup.

In the late 1940s and early 1950s the demand for export crops from the colonial countries boomed. To take advantage of this boom, the Portuguese "recruited" thousands upon thousands of African peasants to work on the coffee, cotton, and sugar plantations. Called *contratados* (contract workers), these plantation hands were subjected to forced labor with little or no pay. According to Basil Davidson in his book *In the Eye of the Storm,* there were 379,000 contratados in 1954. Ten years later, MPLA leader Viriato da Cruz described the extent of this system and its affects on traditional Angolan society in an interview published in the February 15, 1964, *El Moudjahid,* the central organ of the Algerian Front de Libération Nationale (FLN—National Liberation Front):

> These masses comprised around 800,000 workers in the rural zones, subjected to forced labor, around 350,000 Africans living in conditions of underemployment and joblessness in the urban zones, and around 1,000,000 Angolan émigrés, who were submitted in their turn to superexploitation by the Belgians, the English and the South Africans.
>
> In brief, more than 2,000,000 Africans [were] torn from their social and geographical surroundings by the disintegration of the traditional societies, by violence and by the theft of their land, vegetating outside the traditional framework of their lives, in zones of insecurity and despair, deprived of their old ties.

Their migration between the Belgian-ruled Congo and Angola had an important side effect on the contratados. Marcum describes the situation after clashes between Congolese nationalists and the Belgians in January 1959: "First, believing that unemployed Angolan emigres had played an inflammatory role in the rioting, Belgian police arrested and extradited several hundred Angolans during January and February. Many of these repatriates, who were hustled off by Portuguese officials to work on the booming coffee plantations, went back to Angola influenced by nationalist ideas picked up in the Congo. They were soon spreading the word about higher wages north of the border. Angola was thereby further infected with politico-economic discontent" (Marcum, p. 71).

Angolans found jobs in the rapidly expanding ports, the iron and diamond mines, and the small but growing manufacturing sector located near the port cities. About 100,000 Angolans were sent to South Africa each year to work in the mines there. Duffy (p. 189) quotes a 1962 study of Angola by Thomas Okuma, which noted the political influence of this Angolan working class. Okuma said: "The system of 'voluntary labour' has contributed to the spread of nationalism, due to the transportation of workers from the south to the coffee plantations located in the north and to the docks in the two coastal cities of Luanda and Lobito. Workers made contacts beyond their own tribal groups. Their common grievances of inadequate pay and bad working conditions have meant the beginning of a feeling of solidarity against their European employers."

1961: The Explosion

The Portuguese authorities sensed the impending storm as early as 1959. In March of that year they arrested hundreds of Africans, including leaders of the MPLA. Part of the Portuguese air force and 2,000 additional troops were sent to Angola. Again in June 1960 there were mass arrests in Luanda, Lobito, Malange, and Dalatando. In July Portuguese troops began terrorizing the Luanda *muceques* (literally "sandy places," the slums surrounding the city), burning houses and torturing inhabitants. After Agostinho Neto was arrested at his office in Luanda, villagers from his home area marched to the administrative headquarters in Catete in protest. Troops opened fire on the crowd, killing thirty demonstrators. In November, twenty-eight nationalists from Cabinda were slaughtered in a Luanda prison. Although the MPLA continued to function from its exile headquarters in Conakry, Guinea, issuing appeals and protests, the Portuguese repression decimated its local groups within Angola.

In the rural areas, unrest was also reaching a high pitch. In the Baixa do Cassange area east of Malange, about 30,000 African farmers, most of them Mbundus, had been forced to grow cotton for the Belgian-owned Cotonang company. The peasants had to sell their crops at a government-fixed price which was well below that of the world market; the annual income for an African family was US$20 to US$30. A fall in cotton prices in 1960 was followed by a failure of the plantation owners to pay the African peasants. In November and December, the African producers stopped work and refused to pay taxes. Retaliatory beatings and arrests followed, sparking a widespread revolt among Africans.

According to Pélissier, the MPLA, the UPA, and the Congolese Parti de la Solidarité Africaine (African Solidarity Party) may have had some influence among the peasants, although the Cotton Revolt itself was largely spontaneous. Marcum credits the "Maria" religious sect of António Mariano with the leadership of the revolt, which began on a wide scale in January 1961. Marcum writes (p. 125):

"As Maria's War gained momentum and spread from remote border areas, which seem to have enjoyed some weeks of 'independence,' into the heart of Malange district, the administration sounded the alarm. Portuguese planes and troops were rushed in to firebomb and strafe villages and to crush all opposition. . . . Portuguese authority was restored in the area, though at a cost of hundreds, perhaps thousands, of lives."

The Cotton Revolt was just a glimpse of what was to come. On the night of February 3-4, 1961, groups of Africans attacked several Portuguese prisons and installations in Luanda itself, suffering heavy losses. An armed white militia was formed and on February 5, after a funeral for some of the slain Portuguese troops and police, the whites began a bloody massacre of Africans in the muceques. According to Patricia McGowan Pinheiro, more than 3,000 Africans were killed on that day alone. On February 10 there was another attack by a group of Africans, with similar results. ("Politics of a Revolt," in *Angola: A Symposium*).

The MPLA claims that it initiated these attacks, and it dates the beginning of the "national revolution" from February 4, 1961. But according to both Pélissier and Marcum, it is not clear who led the actions, although militants from the MPLA and the other small groups in Luanda may have been involved. Whatever the case, the repression that followed nearly destroyed the MPLA within Angola. The MPLA headquarters in Conakry virtually lost contact with the survivors, some of whom managed to escape Luanda and reach the mountainous Dembos region northeast of Luanda.

Next came the March 1961 insurrection in northern Angola led by the UPA. The date was apparently chosen to coincide with a debate on Angola in the United Nations Security Council. A few weeks before, Holden Roberto told Frantz Fanon (according to Fanon's wife): "Pay close attention to March 15, the day of the debate in the U.N.; some very important things are going to happen in Angola."

According to Marcum (p. 135), the UPA's military preparations had begun in mid-1960. In July of that year, Roberto sent UPA activists to Luanda and Nova Lisboa to agitate among the African troops in the Portuguese army. A handful of noncommissioned officers, as well as some lower-ranking African troops, deserted to the UPA and formed the core of the UPA's future military wing. Several days before March 15, UPA members went into northern Angola to prepare for the uprising. One rally of 3,000 was staged near Nova Caipemba on March 10. As early as March 12 a few African farm workers began attacking their bosses. The UPA claimed it organized strikes by plantation workers preceding the revolt. Although the available evidence indicates that the UPA played the key role in initiating the revolt, it also appears that the explosion was much greater than the UPA leaders had expected. Unlike the isolated actions in Luanda the month before, the March 15 revolt quickly gained a mass character. The Portuguese referred to it as the "Great War."

The initial assaults against plantations and administrative and police posts took the Portuguese by surprise. Voicing battle cries of "UPA" and "Lumumba," the rebels staged guerrilla actions along the northern border area, in Cabinda, and in the Dembos, a Mbundu area with a long tradition of resistance to the Portuguese. According to Pélissier, the revolt in the southern Dembos reached the scale of a minor popular uprising. Ovimbundu *contratodos* on many of the northern plantations also took part in it.

"Since March 15, a large triangular slice of Angola—its base along the Congo frontier and its apex reaching 200 miles south, uncomfortably close to the capital city of Luanda—has come almost completely into the hands of African revolutionaries," Hamilton Fish Armstrong reported in the May 15, 1961, *New York Times Magazine.*

Pélissier says, "The eastern corner of the Congo district [later divided into Zaire and Uíge districts] was now Portuguese in only nine fortified posts; the rest was abandoned to the rebels. The UPA brought forward its commandos unopposed in the north-south central corridor, from the frontier down to the Dembos. It registered its greatest psychological success in forcing the Portuguese into the error of abandoning the powerful fortress of Bembe. . . ."

By June, the UPA began burning coffee crops and destroying plantations in the areas they held in the Congo, Cuanza-Norte, and Luanda districts in an effort to break the economic ties of the Portuguese settlers and force them to abandon the land they held in the north. The Portuguese counterattacks became in part a struggle to regain what could be salvaged of the coffee, which in 1961 was worth about $55 million and accounted for 40 percent of Angola's foreign exchange earnings.

Although the UPA sent emissaries south, it was unsuccessful in spreading the revolt beyond the Bakongo areas except among some of the Mbundu.

The Portuguese reprisals against the rebels—and against the African population as a whole—were barbarous. In the north, the Portuguese air force, with napalm, rockets, and machine guns, indiscriminately bombed and strafed rebels, villagers, and refugee columns. The Portuguese settlers, inflamed by exaggerated horror stories of massacres of whites by the rebels, swiftly organized into a "militia" and moved against the African population.

Duffy, writing shortly after the 1961 uprising, described Lisbon's military campaign in the north:

The conflict was regarded by many Portuguese officials as a war of extermination which must be fought as such. African villages in northern Angola were bombed indiscriminately; other villages captured by Portuguese troops were razed, the male inhabitants executed, and women and children driven into the bush. Certainly the atrocities committed by African guerrillas have been more than matched by those of the 'civilizing' Portuguese columns. The Portuguese have given no quarter. Newspaper accounts quote boastful Portuguese military estimates of how many thousands of 'black animals' have been destroyed. Again it is impossible to calculate the number of African lives lost; estimates range from 10,000 to 30,000. But the number of refugees fleeing across the frontier into the Congo now exceeds 150,000. Many of these survivors arrive mutilated, burnt, and wounded. They have told incredible tales of indiscriminate Portuguese brutality. (p. 221.)

But the massacres were not limited to northern Angola. They were carried out against Mbundu in the Cuanza Valley and even reached some parts of central and southern Angola. The Portuguese claimed they had smashed "terrorist plots" in those areas.

The white terror was just as devastating in the cities. The Reverend Clifford J. Parsons, a Baptist missionary who was in Angola at the time of the insurrection, described the situation this way: "Above all in Luanda, three weeks after the outbreak of the revolt, I was myself the confidant of those who were witnesses to the nightly murder of innocent Africans in the outer suburbs. At that time there was no fighting within a hundred miles of Luanda, yet wanton killing went on in this way, and even in broad daylight" ("The Makings of a Revolt," in *Angola: A Symposium,* p. 72).

In another report, Parsons said: "Thousands of colored people have been slaughtered and mutilated. Each night, the Portuguese secret police have broken into houses and dragged Africans into the streets, where they were shot" (*New York Times,* May 3, 1961).

Pélissier noted, however, that the killings were not entirely at random: ". . . every African *assimilado* regarded as a potential leader was suspect, and many were arrested and some were executed" (p. 182). (The Portuguese used the term *assimilado* to describe those Africans who had been educated and "assimilated" into the Portuguese culture.)

As early as May, a Portuguese officer estimated that 30,000 Africans had been killed. The number of deaths by October 7, when the Portuguese announced that their military operations were "complete," are thought to have been as high as 50,000. Many of the dead were the victims of disease and famine caused by the war.

The Struggle in Exile

The crushing of the revolt, and the massive Portuguese reprisals, drove hundreds of thousands of refugees across the border into the Congo (now Zaïre) and other countries. The estimates of the total number of Angolans in exile in Zaïre, the Republic of the Congo, and Zambia ranged from one million to three million (some had emigrated in search of jobs, and others fled from the fighting that continued sporadically during the decade after the 1961 revolt). The areas of UPA strength within Angola were virtually depopulated by the war. In Zaire district, for instance, there were 102,777 inhabitants in 1960; by 1968 this figure had dropped to around 30,000. The forced migrations of the Bakongo and the continued Portuguese repression in northern Angola forced the UPA to base itself among the Bakongo exiles, principally in Congo.

The UPA continued to carry out guerrilla operations in Angola from its base across the border. According to Marcum, the UPA still controlled an area along the northern frontier that was 150 miles wide and 200 miles deep as of January 1962, several months after the Portuguese announced that they had "crushed" the revolt. One indication of the continued guerrilla activity—and the Portuguese reprisals—was the steady stream of refugees that poured into the Congo throughout the mid-1960s.

The UPA's prestige rose greatly as a result of the 1961 revolt. Other nationalist groups and currents in exile or still within Angola were attracted to it. Discussions were held among some of these groups with the aim of reaching agreement on a common course of action against the Portuguese. The MPLA, which was still composed of a small number of intellectuals without a significant following, acknowledged that the UPA had a mass base and made overtures toward "unity" with it. Several attempts were made by the UPA and MPLA in this direction, but with no success. It appears that Roberto may have feared a merger since the MPLA, though small, had educated and able organizers who could have posed a future challenge to his leadership. Roberto's attitude was matched by the MPLA's factional approach. For instance, Marcum writes that on August 8, 1962, Agostinho Neto "dispatched a letter to Roberto in which he referred to and implicitly accepted earlier accusations of racism, sectarianism, tribalism, and treason leveled against Roberto" and his group. (Two days later Neto held a news conference in which he again called for "unity" with Roberto's forces.)

While Roberto was unwilling to join with the MPLA, he did take measures to win the alliance of other groups. In March 1962 the UPA joined with the Partido Democrático de Angola (PDA—Angolan Democratic Party), a small group based among the Bazombo people of northern Angola, to form the Angolan National Liberation Front (FNLA). Before allying with the UPA, the PDA leaders had considered working in a common front with both the MPLA and UPA, but were suspicious of the MPLA leadership. According to Marcum, "they expected that Lisbon, should it ever agree to the principle of self-determination, would use the period of political transition to build up the position of both the MPLA and 'southerners,' because it would consider these two groups to be Portuguese in cultural orientation" (p. 236).

In April 1962 the newly created FNLA, seeking to capitalize on its prestige, formed the Angolan Revolutionary Government in Exile (GRAE—Govêrno Revolucionário de Angola no Exílo). Roberto also sought to broaden the group's ethnic appeal by bringing non-Bakongos into the leadership of the FNLA and GRAE. Jonas Malheiro Savimbi, an Ovimbundu student leader who was later to play an important role on his own, was named foreign minister of the GRAE; he had already been appointed secretary-general of the UPA in late 1961. Rosário Neto, a Mbundu, was the UPA's vice-president, João Batista, a Cuanhama (Ovambo), became a field commander within Angola of the Exército de Libertação Nacional de Angola (ELNA—Angolan National Liberation Army), and Marcos Kassanga, a Ganguela, was appointed its chief of staff in Léopoldville. But despite these efforts to broaden the leadership, the FNLA remained predominantly Bakongo at its base.

The FNLA also had a trade union group, the General League of Angolan Workers (LGTA—Liga General dos Trabalhadores de Angola). According to Marcum (p. 304), it was probably considerably larger than any of the other exile Angolan union organizations. The LGTA set up local affiliates within Angola, the function of which, Marcum writes, "was to popularize the concept of trade unionism among former farm laborers and other workers through local committees, using mimeographed material sent inside from LGTA headquarters in Léopoldville" (pp. 304, 305). The LGTA also made an abortive attempt to organize the workers at the diamond mines in northeastern Angola.

Before the Congo won its independence from Belgium, the UPA's activities were officially banned in that country. But the

UPA maintained ties with Lumumba until his assassination, and the support of other Congolese nationalist leaders saved the UPA from serious Belgian interference. When Joseph Kasavubu, the leader of the Congolese Abako (Alliance des Bakongo), became president of the new Congo Republic he turned against the UPA. Apparently seeing it as a rival for the support of Bakongos living in the Congo, the Abako threatened and harassed the UPA's members. The French daily *Le Monde* reported on June 28, 1961, that Kasavubu, General Joseph Mobutu, and another anti-Lumumba Congolese leader had considered expelling the UPA from the Congo to avoid Portuguese retaliation. At the same time, the Abako assisted the MPLA and its refugee relief organization.

In August 1961 Cyrille Adoula, a personal friend of Roberto, was recognized as prime minister, and the UPA was once again able to function from the Congo with relative freedom. It was allowed to open training camps in Congolese territory, and in June 1963 the Adoula regime recognized the GRAE.

The coming to power of Moïse Tshombe in July 1964 was another setback for the FNLA in using the Congo as a base for its operations. Roberto described the harassment of his group in a 1965 interview with *Révolution Africaine,* a weekly journal of the Algerian FLN: "The obvious collusion of the Portuguese with Tshombe had grave consequences for us: confiscation of arms and munitions, acts of intimidation and harassment, blocking of the Angolan-Congolese border, tacitly giving the right to pursuit to the Portuguese army against our refugees on Congolese territory. Attacks against our rear bases, suppression of our radio broadcasts, open activity of the Portuguese secret police (PIDE) [Polícia Internacional e de Defesa do Estado—International State Security Police] in the Congo."

On January 25, 1965, Roberto attempted to leave the Congo to visit Lusaka, capital of Zambia, at the invitation of President Kenneth Kaunda. But according to a GRAE statement, he was formally forbidden from doing so by Tshombe's secret police. Despite these difficulties, the FNLA and GRAE remained based in the Congo, according to the GRAE, because of logistics advantages and the presence of the refugee population. With the ouster of Tshombe in October 1965 and the coming to power of General Joseph Mobutu, the pressure on the FNLA eased somewhat. It later managed to get aid from the Mobutu regime.

The FNLA and MPLA were not only rivals for leadership of the Angolan independence struggle; they also attempted to outbid each other in their campaign for foreign recognition and support. One of the most common weapons in this competition was the use of slander. The FNLA, for instance, sought to disparage the MPLA by labeling it a "Communist" organization. The MPLA, in turn, denounced the FNLA as "tribalist," "racist," or a "puppet of U.S. imperialism." At one point the MPLA even accused Roberto of "vanity" for refusing to mention in public "the great patriot and fighter Dr. Agostinho Neto." The MPLA could claim few achievements within Angola at that time, and had to place particular reliance on such name-calling in its bid to prevent the FNLA from gaining a monopoly on outside assistance.

Slanders of the FNLA had been circulated by the MPLA and other groups since the beginning of the 1960s. On December 16, 1964, Moscow joined the campaign to discredit the FNLA. An article in *Pravda* claimed that the GRAE was linked with U.S. imperialism and with the Tshombe regime. These stories were repeated, with many embellishments, in other countries over the years, particularly by the pro-Moscow Communist parties. The Portuguese authorities took an interest in this bickering and also sought to enter the fray for their own purposes. For instance, João Baptista Nunes Pereira Neto hinted in an essay titled "Movimentos Subversivos de Angola" (published in *Angola,* a Salazarist handbook) that the UPA was backed by the CIA and the MPLA by the KGB. His aim was to prove that the Angolan rebels had no base within the country and only survived thanks to foreign backing.

It appears that Roberto did have some illusions in the early 1960s that Washington would put pressure on Lisbon to negotiate with the nationalist forces. For instance, in an interview published in the June 6, 1975, *Le Monde,* Roberto said: "When I was in the United States, I greatly admired President Kennedy, whom I met before his election. It was in 1961 that, for the first and last time, the Americans voted against Portugal in the [United Nations] Security Council. I returned to the United States in 1963, on the day of Kennedy's assassination. I couldn't meet him again. I have not set foot on American oil since then. I have never received aid from the United States."

As the recent revelations of the CIA's early involvement in Angola have shown, Roberto was lying about U.S. aid. But the limited amounts of CIA money the FNLA got did not prevent Roberto from realizing which side Washington was really backing in Angola and from publicly denouncing it. In January

1964 Roberto said: "I came to the conclusion that the Western countries are hypocritical. They help our enemies. While paying lip service to self-determination, the United States supplies its North Atlantic treaty's ally, Portugal, with arms that are used to kill us" (*New York Times,* January 4, 1964.) He also noted that G. Mennen Williams, assistant secretary of state for African affairs, had tried to convince the Congolese regime not to recognize the GRAE.

Nor did the CIA money prevent the FNLA from condemning Washington's aggression in other parts of the world. As early as July 8, 1965, Johnny Eduardo, the head of the offical GRAE mission in Algeria, issued a statement condemning President Johnson's escalation of the Vietnam War and Washington's plans to bomb Hanoi. A few months earlier, Eduardo said in an interview with *Révolution Africaine,* "The struggle of the Cuban, Vietnamese and Chinese peoples, for example, are a great inspiration to us."

Holden Roberto has frequently declared that the FNLA would accept aid from any source, as long as no political conditions were attached. Nor does the acceptance of aid from imperialist sources, even the United States, necessarily make a nationalist group an "imperialist puppet." Nationalist movements frequently seek to exploit whatever contradictions exist among the world powers to achieve their objectives. In their struggle against Portuguese colonialism, the Angolan rebels were compelled to follow a policy of seeking material aid, including weapons, from any available source. They had every right to do so.

The U.S. imperialists, of course, hope to gain political concessions, or future influence in return for such aid. They have no interest whatever in allowing a national liberation struggle to achieve its final goal: the ending of all foreign domination, including that of the United States. They would do everything in their power to prevent that. It would thus be a dangerous error for a nationalist organization to grant political or economic concessions, either to Washington or to other imperialist sources of aid, since that could jeopardize the aims of the entire independence struggle.

It should further be noted that making political concessions to such a source of aid as Moscow or Peking could also harm a nationalist struggle. Although the Soviet Union and the People's Republic of China are not imperialist, the ruling Stalinist bureaucracies in Moscow and Peking have their own foreign policy interests to advance. In exchange for Washington's "friendship," they do their best to keep the lid on revolutionary movements around the world. (This policy currently goes under the label détente.) Although they give limited aid to struggles from time to time, the bureaucracies are always prepared to use these struggles as a bartering point with imperialism.

In any case, most of the FNLA's backing, at least before 1975, came from sources other than the United States. In the early 1960s the FNLA had ties with the Nkrumah regime in Ghana. FNLA officers were trained in Algeria by the FLN under Ben Bella, and in 1964 the Algerian regime recognized the GRAE (it later changed its position and supported both the FNLA and MPLA, calling for their unification). The FNLA received some aid from the Tunisian regime. The Organization of African Unity (OAU) recognized the GRAE in 1964, but lifted the recognition in June 1971, sending some aid to both the FNLA and MPLA and pressing for their unification.

On January 3, 1964, Roberto announced that the FNLA had decided to accept aid from Peking, which it received off and on for more than a decade thereafter. He said the FNLA would also accept aid from "other Communist countries." According to Nicolas Vieira of the FNLA in an interview published in the February 15, 1964, *El Moudjahid,* "We have increased armaments available thanks to the support of friendly socialist countries, Yugoslavia, the Soviet Union and People's China." The Soviet aid was presumably halted at the time of the *Pravda* attack on the FNLA later that year. According to Kenneth L. Adelman, writing in the April 1975 *Foreign Affairs,* the FNLA also received medical supplies from the World Council of Churches and the World Health Organization in the early 1970s.

Unlike the MPLA and the UNITA, which use socialist rhetoric, the FNLA claims that it is purely nationalist, with no "ideology." For instance, Henrick Vaal Neto, an FNLA representative during the negotiations with Lisbon in January 1975, said, according to the January 14, 1975, Lisbon daily *República:* "The FNLA has always tried to avoid affiliation with any ideological bloc. We think the Angolan people are mature enough to delineate their own ideology, always according to the Angolan reality. . . . What interests us Angolans, in respect to ideology, has nothing to do with 'isms.' "

Despite the FNLA's lack of the kind of perspective for the Angolan independence struggle that could lead it to a successful conclusion—the ouster of all imperialist interests from the country and the overthrow of capitalism—it was still the only nationalist organization in the early 1960s that had any kind of mass base and was actively fighting against the Portuguese colonialists.

The Marxist assessment of this question was sketched in a February 17, 1964, statement by the United Secretariat of the Fourth International. It noted the FNLA's active opposition to Portuguese rule and its participation in mass struggles. "The most effective way in which revolutionary Marxists can help the Angolan freedom fighters find their way to the program of socialism is to participate actively in the struggles led by the FNLA, to help them obtain material support in fighting against Portuguese imperialism, and to back them in resisting every neocolonialist maneuver, above all those emanating from American imperialism."

Livio Maitan, a leader of the Fourth International, pointed out in an article in the March 5, 1965, issue of *Intercontinental Press*:

> As for the arguments being circulated about this or that Angolan leader rumored to be "an agent of American imperialism" or a "friend of Tshombe," we repeat once again that aside from the fact that no serious proof has been offered up to now, this would not be of decisive importance. The real problem is to ascertain whether or not there is a movement that is struggling, whether it exercises proponderant influence among the masses at a given stage. If these conditions hold, then it is the duty of revolutionists to display active solidarity with those who are struggling, independently of the attitude or possible orientation of a leader or even of an entire leadership. . . . While not pretending to remain aloof from the fray like pious preachers, they do not believe they are called on to mix into every factional dispute that develops.

During the early 1960s the FNLA was the only group carrying out any significant actions within Angola; the MPLA was in virtual disarray. The Portuguese repression had eliminated most of its leaders in Luanda and other cities, and the survivors in the countryside had to contend with the Portuguese troops as well as hostile FNLA guerrillas, who, in their own factional interest, attempted to physically prevent the MPLA from establishing a base within Angola. On occasion, FNLA forces even ambushed and killed MPLA guerrillas.

The MPLA was cut off from much of the Angolan exile

community when the Adoula regime officially expelled the MPLA from the Congo in November of 1963 and the FNLA barred MPLA guerrillas from crossing Congolese territory to reinforce the remaining MPLA rebels within Angola. This setback came on top of the OAU conciliation committee's recommendation in July 1963 to the OAU member-states to recognize the GRAE.

The MPLA tried to bolster its image by forming the Frente Democrática para a Libertação de Angola (FDLA—Angolan Democratic Liberation Front) in 1963 with several other groups. That move, however, did further damage to the MPLA's reputation, since some of the groups in the FDLA had openly collaborated with the Portuguese colonialists. The Ntobako Angola, a small Bakongo grouping, had provided the Portuguese with information about the UPA. Writing of Ntobako leader Angelino Alberto's visit to New York City in 1962, Marcum reports: "His trip was sponsored by the Portuguese-American Committee on Foreign Affairs, registered as a foreign agent with the Department of Justice. To the press, Alberto denounced nationalist violence in Angola and released pictures showing himself addressing peaceful Angolan villagers, who were in turn surrounded by Portuguese military personnel" (p. 231). Another of the Bakongo groups in the FDLA, the Ngwizako (Ngwizani a Kongo), also had collaborated with the Portuguese, leading military patrols to the sites of UPA-controlled villages in northern Angola. The MPLA leaders soon realized that an alliance with such collaborationist groups would do little to build their organization or gain African backing. They allowed the FDLA to fade out.

The reverses experienced by the MPLA heightened differences within the organization. It began to fragment. In December 1962 Viriato Da Cruz, one of the MPLA's principal founders, left after having failed to unify it with the UPA. The majority of the MPLA's members also left. For a while, Cruz declared that his group represented the MPLA, but on April 22, 1964, he joined the FNLA. Mário Pintó de Andrade resigned from the leadership of the MPLA in July 1963. Agostinho Neto and Lucio Lara then gained control of its central leadership.

After its expulsion from Kinshasa, the MPLA moved its exile headquarters to Brazzaville, Republic of the Congo. "A conference of some fifty MPLA leaders at Brazzaville from January 3 to 10, 1964, took stock of the situation," Pélissier writes. "They had only two or three hundred soldiers left." Since the MPLA was

ANGOLA (perspective view looking eastward): Resources, main ethnic groups, and traditional base areas of nationalist organizations

43

blocked from moving its forces into northern Angola, it sent a few guerrillas into Cabinda in January 1963. But the Brazzaville regime of Fulbert Youlou hampered the MPLA's activities, its policy being to support the Cabindan separatists of the Movimento de Libertação do Enclave de Cabinda (MLEC—Cabindan Liberation Movement).

Shortly after its internal crisis, the MPLA's fortunes rose. The Youlou regime was overthrown in 1964 by Alphonse Massamba-Débat, who allowed the MPLA to function more freely from the Congo Republic. The MPLA also continued its search for material aid from other countries. Despite its denunciations of the FNLA for receiving American aid, the MPLA was itself not opposed to looking toward the imperialist countries for help; in 1963 Neto visited the United States to solicit such backing. Speaking before the United Nations on October 24, 1975, Saydi Mingas, a leader of the MPLA, noted that the MPLA had approached Washington for arms with which to fight the Portuguese but had been turned down (as reported in the October 25, 1975, issue of the Lisbon *O Século*).

In 1964 Neto visited Moscow, with more favorable results. From the Soviet statements attacking the FNLA and picturing the MPLA as the only significant Angolan liberation group, it is clear that Neto obtained not only financial support, but also Moscow's political backing. The MPLA also maintained contacts with the Portuguese Communist and Socialist parties. According to Pélissier (p. 216), the MPLA had a military training camp at Brazzaville organized by Cubans. He notes that at one time the MPLA also received some backing from Peking (p. 211). The MPLA managed to gain the support of various liberal and left-wing forces in Europe, primarily because of its Soviet backing and its effective propaganda apparatus.

In 1964 the MPLA stepped up its actions in Cabinda. It also moved a few leaders into sparsely populated eastern Angola, where they began military operations in May 1966 and attempted to win the backing of the peoples in that region. The MPLA had maintained its support among the Mbundu in the Dembos area and along the Luanda-Malange corridor. In June and July of 1966 the MPLA managed to send a column of 150 to 200 rebels through FNLA-controlled territory into the Dembos region to strengthen its forces. From 1967 to 1969, the MPLA moved part of its military and political staff to Lusaka, Zambia, and then into eastern Angola itself. The Kaunda regime in Lusaka gave the

MPLA some material aid, but threatened to cut it off if the MPLA forces attacked the Benguela railway, which Lusaka used to transport its copper to the Angolan port of Lobito. By 1970, the MPLA claimed to be carrying out guerrilla actions in the Dembos area and in the districts of Cabinda, Moxico, Cuando-Cubango, Lunda, Malange, and Bié.

While the MPLA's military claims were undoubtedly exaggerated, as were those of the FNLA and the UNITA, it is clear that by the late 1960s the MPLA had become a significant Angolan nationalist group and was actively opposing the Portuguese colonialists. The OAU recognized this fact when it lifted its sole recognition of the GRAE in 1971 and sent aid to both the FNLA and MPLA.

While the MPLA was recovering and starting to become active, the FNLA faced a series of internal crises of its own. The pressures of trying to lead a struggle from exile resulted in splits from the FNLA and GRAE, and Roberto's plans to broaden the FNLA's ethnic base fell apart. There were defections from the UPA and FNLA to the MPLA, primarily of Mbundus. Shortly after the 1961 uprising in the north, the Mbundu rebels in the Dembos region, who had originally been organized by the UPA, switched their allegiance to the MPLA. This hardening of the ethnic divisions between the two groups heightened the already existing factional rivalries. Noting the military clashes between the two groups, Marcum wrote, "Significantly, their sporadic armed encounters always occurred in either the Lower Congo-Angola frontier region, which was vital for access to the fighting zones in northern Angola, or in ethnic transition zones such a Nambuangongo, where political and ethnic rivalry were most likely to reinforce one another" (p. 219).

In 1962, Marcos Kassanga and André Kassinda (an Ovimbundu leader of the FNLA's trade union group) left the organization, charging it with "tribalism." The most prominent Ovimbundu leader of the GRAE, Jonas Savimbi, resigned as foreign affairs minister and left the organization in July 1964. He was joined by José João Liahuca, an Ovimbundu director of the GRAE refugee aid service. Both denounced the GRAE's alleged inefficiency, lack of unity, inadequate support to the rebels within Angola, and "tribalism."

This crisis led to a slump in the FNLA's military activities for several years. Beginning in 1968, however, its guerrilla actions were stepped up once again, and between 1968 and 1970 the

FNLA's structure was reorganized. In 1970, the FNLA's two components, the UPA and PDA, were dissolved and the FNLA reconstituted as a party. The FNLA claimed credit for guerrilla actions in the districts of Cabinda, Zaire, Uíge, Cuanza-Norte, Luanda, and Malange, with occasional forays into Lunda and Moxico.

Another Contender Enters the Field

The third main Angolan liberation group, the UNITA, was formed by Jonas Savimbi in 1965. The UNITA is based predominantly on the Ovimbundu population of the central plateau region, but also has adherents among the smaller ethnic groupings of eastern and southern Angola. According to Marcum (pp. 118-119), members of the Chokwe, Luvale, and Luchzai ethnic associations (called, respectively Ukwashi wa Chokwe, Chijilochalimbo, and Vilinga va Kambungo) were absorbed into the UNITA in 1966.

The UNITA's first guerrilla action was in December 1966, when 500 UNITA troops attacked the frontier town of Teixeira de Sousa on the Benguela Railway, losing about half their forces. In 1969, after the UNITA derailed a freight train, the Kaunda regime, under the pressure of a temporary Portuguese closure of the railway, expelled Savimbi from Zambia. He then moved his entire headquarters into eastern Angola.

An OAU commission visited eastern Angola in 1968, but found little evidence that the UNITA was very active. However, the UNITA's strength appears to have increased by 1973, according to *Washington Post* correspondent Leon Dash, who visited UNITA-controlled territory that year. Dash reported that thousands of Angolan peasants were living in UNITA-organized villages. "The UNITA guerrillas," he said, ". . . administer, apparently effectively, what appears to be a substantial area in eastern Angola." The UNITA rebels claimed that they were fighting in Moxico, Bié, Cuando-Cubango, Huila, Lunda, and Huambo districts in central, eastern, and southern Angola.

According to António Fernandes, the UNITA's secretary of information and publicity, in an interview published in the October 1974 issue of *Black World,* the UNITA was formed by dissidents from both the FNLA and MPLA who were opposed to trying to lead the independence struggle from exile. The UNITA program was essentially similar to those of the FNLA and

MPLA. Among other things, it called for Angola's independence, the "emancipation of Angolan women," a "planned economy to meet all the needs of our population and to construct an industrialized country," the "abolition of the forced labor system and other forms of exploitation of physical labour in the country," the "liquidation of all foreign bases in Angola," and "co-operation to the fullest extent with all National Liberation Movements in Africa and all progressive forces the world over to get rid of all forms of foreign domination from our continent." (The program was published in 1968 in a UNITA pamphlet called *Angola—Seventh Year.*)

According to Savimbi, all the UNITA's weapons were captured from the Portuguese or in clashes with the MPLA and FNLA. Savimbi also claimed that the UNITA received no military or economic aid from any foreign state, although Dash noted that it did get some aid from the World Council of Churches and the U.S.-based African Liberation Support Committee. In addition, Savimbi was reported to have visited Peking in 1968 and to have received a small amount of Chinese aid. Savimbi also told Dash that he had requested, in separate letters to the MPLA and FNLA, to join the Supreme Liberation Council, but was rejected. (The council was set up in December 1972 in an effort to unite the MPLA and FNLA but soon fell apart.)

Both the MPLA and FNLA have charged that the UNITA collaborated with the Portuguese forces during the colonial war. These charges stem from a series of four "letters" published in the July 8, 1974, issue of the Paris magazine *Afrique-Asie,* which backs the MPLA politically. The "letters," purportedly written by Savimbi and two Portuguese officers in 1972, discussed carrying out military actions against the MPLA. On July 19, 1974, António Fernandes, UNITA secretary of information, issued a communiqué from Lusaka stating that they were forgeries.

Like the MPLA, the UNITA attempted to give its nationalist program a "socialist" coloring, perhaps to aid in its search for backing from Moscow or Peking or to differentiate itself from the other two groups on an ostensibly political basis rather than a factional or ethnic one. Many of its military and propaganda statements, at least until the 1974 Portuguese coup, were laced with Maoist terminology and rhetoric. The UNITA even went to the point of adopting a concept of a "people's war" based on the peasantry similar to Mao's.

Dash reported the following after a discussion of the UNITA's long-term strategy with Savimbi: "The guerrillas' strategy in the first stage of the war, he said, is to persuade more and more of the African population to join them in the forests, thus isolating the towns. In the second stage, which is to come when the guerrillas have won over enough of the peasant population, they plan to attack the towns—which by then will be occupied primarily by the Portuguese, according to the plan." Savimbi said, "We are in a war that might last for generations." In the interview in *Black World,* Fernandes also declared that the UNITA was formed "within the Marxism/Leninism lines" and that the UNITA was aiming for a "socialist" regime in Angola after independence. Wilson Santos, a member of the UNITA's political bureau, later clarified this point. According to a February 18, 1975, Agence France-Presse dispatch, he said that the UNITA "wants to build a Socialist society" in Angola—not one modeled on China, Senegal, or Congo Republic, but one that "fits in with the history and realities of our country." In saying that, Santos was simply echoing the "African socialist" concept propounded by such figures as Julius K. Nyerere of Tanzania and Leopold Sedor Senghor of Senegal. The "African socialism" advanced by them is little more than a rhetorical disguise for the fact that their countries are still dominated by imperialist economic interests.

A New Challenge:
Portuguese Neocolonialism

Before the April 25, 1974, coup in Lisbon, the independence forces in Guinea-Bissau had scored major military and political gains, and in Mozambique they were rapidly escalating their activities. But in Angola, after the crushing of the 1961 rebellions, the direct pressure against Portuguese colonial rule was limited to occasional ambushes and sporadic clashes in the countryside. There were almost no strike actions or other visible signs of unrest in the cities. A united and effective campaign against Portuguese rule was seriously undermined by the rivalries between the MPLA, FNLA, and UNITA.

However, the limited warfare in Angola combined with the more significant campaigns in Guinea-Bissau and Mozambique was an economic and political drain on Lisbon, tying up 150,000 troops in Africa. Military expenditures comprised up to 50 percent of the Portuguese government's budget in some years. According to Portuguese Socialist Party leader Mário Soares, the wars in the colonies cost more than $6 billion.

These wars fostered the spread of antiwar sentiments, both among civilians and within the ranks of the army itself. The growing opposition to the colonial wars came at a time of economic crisis, with high inflation and unemployment. These factors greatly increased discontent within Portugal, and lead to the overthrow of the Salazarist dictatorship of Marcelo Caetano in the April 1974 military coup.

The Lisbon coup, in turn, affected the course of the Angolan liberation struggle. It brought the prospects of formal independence closer, raised the conflict to a more clearly political level, heightened the anticolonial sentiment throughout the country, and drew broader sections of the Angolan population into active opposition to the Portuguese imperialists. Above all, it shifted the focus of the independence movement away from the rural areas. The struggle for control of the cities began.

The coup marked a realization by the Portuguese bourgeoisie that it could not hold on to its colonial empire by force alone, a conclusion that the French, British, and Belgian ruling classes had drawn in relation to their African colonies more than a decade before. For the new military rulers in Lisbon, organized in the Movimento das Forças Armadas (MFA—Armed Forces Movement), the immediate need was to find a "solution" that could end the wars while allowing the Portuguese imperialists to retain their economic interests in Africa. The MFA's initial aim was not even to grant formal independence to its colonies, but to hang on as long as possible through maneuvers, compromises, and threats.

One version of Lisbon's neocolonial strategy was put forward by General António de Spínola. His book, *Portugal e o Futuro* (*Portugal and the Future*), published in Lisbon in February 1974, two months before the coup, outlined his proposals for the future relations between Lisbon and its colonies: the creation of a federation of four supposedly equal states, in which Lisbon would dictate policies in the areas of foreign affairs, defense, and finances. Shortly after the coup, he summed up his policy in a sentence: "Self-determination," he told reporters, "should not be confused with independence."

Even without Spínola's clarification, none of the African rebel groups were confused by what he meant by "self-determination." All three demanded independence. On the day of the coup, Agostinho Neto declared in Ottawa, Canada, that Spínola's formula as outlined in his book "doesn't suit us. . . . This coup," he said, "does not mean that we will obtain independence." An MPLA representative in Algiers said a few days later, "The MPLA states its readiness to negotiate with Portugal the question of the complete independence of our country." Roberto declared from his headquarters in Kinshasa after the coup that any formula for federation or autonomy "is outdated." He added, "What we want is that power in Angola be returned to the majority."

The May 2, 1974, *Le Monde* published a communiqué of the UNITA, which said: "The Portuguese colonial-fascist regime is losing its wars in Africa, and angry officers have overthrown the

Caetano government. Heading the coup is the famous General Spinola, a veteran of the battle of Leningrad [as an observer with the Nazi forces during World War II] and hangman of the peoples of Angola and Guinea-Bissau.

"This rebel general is right to recognize that Portugal cannot win with the methods that have been used up to now. What he has yet to discover is that Portugal cannot win by any other method or reform."

Following this immediate rebuff by the Angolan nationalists, as well as by Frelimo and the PAIGC (Partido Africano da Independência da Guiné-Bissau e Cabo Verde—African Party for the Independence of Guinea-Bissau and the Cape Verde Islands), the MFA tried a mixture of saber rattling and verbal compromise. On May 6 General Francisco da Costa Gomes made a cease-fire offer, calling on the African nationalists to lay down their arms and accept the "framework of the democratic program of the armed forces." Costa Gomes added that unless an agreement was reached, "Portugal will have no other choice than to continue the war."

Two weeks later an MFA representative added another inducement to the rebels, offering to organize a referendum in the colonies so that the populations could exercise "their right to self-determination." Costa Gomes, in an interview in the June 1, 1974, issue of the South African weekly *The Point*, specified what such a Portuguese-organized referendum would be designed to accomplish. "I am convinced that Angola will decide to remain Portuguese. It should strengthen its relations with South Africa and Rhodesia."

The three Angolan nationalist groups, realizing that such a referendum would be little more than a farce, repeated their rejections of the MFA's "offers."

A UNITA representative said at a news conference in Brussels August 29: "We cannot negotiate independence and this is why we refuse General António de Spínola's proposal to organize a referendum. It is out of the question. We have been fighting fourteen years for the principle of independence."

Neto, in an interview published in the May 27 issue of the Algerian daily *El Moudjahid*, stated: "For our people, the referendum solution is not acceptable. We reject a referendum organized by the Portuguese and carried out in Angola by the administration, the army, and the police. Because of that, it would not guarantee a serious result. We demand that Portugal

purely and simply put an end to its domination of our country.
The referendum would be no more than a means used by the
Portuguese to prolong their presence in our country."

Roberto stated in July: "We will step up our operations. This is
the only alternative for our group. We will fight for another
thirteen years if necessary."

In an attempt to get one or more of the nationalist groups to
break ranks and accept his proposals, Spínola also tried to pit
them against each other. In June, Lisbon officials said they
would begin negotiations with those liberation movements
"present within the country," a definition that from Lisbon's
viewpoint included only the UNITA. They noted that "all other
armed groups of African liberation movements have their
headquarters in Kinshasa, Brazzaville, and Lusaka," an obvious
reference to the MPLA and FNLA. Furthermore, in his secret
meeting with Zaïre President Mobutu Sese Seko on September 14,
Spínola may have solicited help in pressuring the FNLA into
accepting Lisbon's schemes.

To strengthen his hand, Spínola enlisted the help of the
Portuguese Socialist and Communist parties, which had accepted
posts in the military junta's cabinet. SP head Mário Soares, as
foreign minister, played a particularly important role in trying to
sell the Spínola package to the African independence fighters.
After a long meeting with a Frelimo delegation in Zambia June 5,
Soares declared that "the problem of winding up nearly 500 years
of rule by Portugal over her East African possession was
complex."

On June 11 Spínola delivered a speech in which he said that
"immediate independence would be a loud negation of the
generally accepted democratic principles" of the MFA. According
to a *New York Times* dispatch from Lisbon on the same day,
"The Labor Minister, Avelino António Pacheco Gonçalves, a
Communist, gave tacit approval to General Spinola's declaration,
saying that the broad principles had been agreed to by the parties
in the Provisional Government."

Spínola also had a few other cards to play in his search for a
winning formula in Angola. After the coup there emerged in
Angola several small groups claiming to be a third force.
Frequently led by white settlers, these groups openly favored
solutions such as those put forward by Spínola, so he hoped to
use them as a counterweight to the MPLA, FNLA, and UNITA.
The most important of these was the Frente Unidade Angolana

(FUA—Angolan Unity Front), led by Fernando Falção, a white businessman from Lobito who was brought into the colonial administration in September 1974.

The white settler population of Angola, estimated at about 500,000, was twice the size of that in Mozambique, for example. Many of them were unskilled or semiskilled workers who had emigrated from Portugal to Angola to escape unemployment. They were thus less willing to leave the colony than the settlers in Mozambique, many of whom were highly skilled workers, technicians, and managers. The Portuguese imperialists may also have calculated that the Angolan settlers would be more intransigent in their opposition to the Black nationalists since their jobs would be more immediately threatened by African workers after formal independence took effect.

In an attempt to terrorize the African community and blunt the developing nationalist upsurge in Angola, white gangs launched armed raids into Luanda's Black muceques in July and August 1974. Hundreds of Africans were killed and thousands fled to the countryside.

What the white settlers—and the Portuguese administration in Luanda—did not expect was the African response to these attacks. The rightist terror raids against the African population met with a reaction that signaled the potential power of Angola's urban masses. In an article written July 20, 1974, the famous Peruvian peasant leader Hugo Blanco described part of this response:

> In view of the fact that the actions of white terrorists continued with the approval of the white police, on July 15 a column of 5,000 Black soldiers and officials was formed. They marched on the military headquarters to ask that they be permitted to protect the Black communities. General Franco Pinheiro was forced to accept this request. Meanwhile, Black civilians who had accompanied the soldiers and who were arrested en route, were being attacked by the police.

> On the same day, there were many incidents in Black communities where the population responded to attacks by burning down the stores of white businessmen.

> Also that day there was a general strike of Black workers, as a sign of mourning and protest. In spite of the strong police repression, the strike was a success. Strike pickets were prevented from being present at workplaces, so they stationed themselves on the outskirts of the Black neighborhoods.

> During the afternoon the burial of five victims of white terrorism took place. The funeral march left from the Liga Nacional Africana and was

accompanied by more than 20,000 persons, many whites among them. There were banners of the liberation movements in Angola and the other colonies, and singing of the MPLA anthem and religious songs in the Kimbundu dialect. (*Intercontinental Press*, September 9, 1974.)

The day after the Luanda strike, a crowd of Africans marched to the governor's palace. In some muceques the Africans took control, forming self-defense groups, driving out the white settlers, and blocking entry to the white gangs. With the departure of the white shopkeepers from the muceques, the inhabitants in some cases formed neighborhood committees to organize the distribution of food and other services.

Many other African mobilizations occurred following the Lisbon coup. During May, for example, Africans took to the streets in Luanda in opposition to the MFA's "self-determination" schemes. Thousands mobilized May 26. The May 30, 1974, London *Guardian* described the protest: "Thousands of black Angolans streamed through central Luanda a few days ago waving placards and shouting support for immediate independence—the biggest demonstration in the territory since the revolution."

The following day General Franco Pinheiro banned all demonstrations and rejected a demand by African protesters that he disarm the white settlers.

The Lisbon coup also touched off a strike wave in Angola that lasted more than a year. The Angolan workers, whose wage demands had been suppressed for years by the colonial authorities, suddenly saw an opportunity to better their lot. Within weeks of the coup, workers started walking off their jobs, particularly in such key sectors as the British-owned Benguela railway and at the ports of Luanda and Lobito. The May 31, 1974, London *Guardian* described one of the first walkouts: "In Angola, a strike by 13,000 workers of the Benguela Railway Company has paralysed the 840-mile line between Zambia and Lobito. The workers are demanding pay increases ranging from 50 to 100 per cent." The June 8 Luanda weekly *Notícia* reported a strike by the Luanda dockers, who were demanding higher wages and better working conditions. Both the railway workers and the dockers repeatedly went out on strike during the next several months. Trade unions had been virtually nonexistent among African laborers. Now they formed workers' committees in some industries to organize strike actions and to put forward their demands.

It was against this background that the Angolan nationalists pressed their campaign against the continued presence of the Portuguese forces in Angola. The FNLA in particular carried out much of the fighting that took place after the Lisbon coup. It increased its recruitment and training of Angolan exiles in Zaïre and began to move them steadily into the Bakongo region in northern Angola that had been its traditional base of support. In June 1974, 250 Chinese military instructors arrived in Kinshasa to train FNLA troops. In August, the Libyan regime began to send aid to the FNLA.

By the end of August, at least two full-scale attacks by the FNLA on Portuguese military forces and eight other raids in the Carmona region had been reported. The Lisbon daily *A Capital* reported August 14 that ten FNLA guerrillas had been killed; the August 20 issue noted that thirteen Portuguese soldiers had died since the beginning of the month. The Portuguese, who estimated the FNLA forces fighting in the north at about 5,000, launched search and destroy missions against the FNLA rebels. By October 1, the FNLA claimed that it had captured a number of important towns in the north, including Carmona, and was stepping up its offensive.

The Angolan nationalists did not limit themselves to guerrilla actions in the countryside. Realizing the significance of the unrest in the cities, the MPLA, FNLA, and UNITA each sought to establish an urban base.

In contending for political influence among urban Angolans, the MPLA appears to have had a head start over its two main rivals. According to Pélissier, the MPLA, in the late 1960s when it was increasing its guerrilla actions in several parts of the countryside, also began to rebuild its clandestine cells in some cities. "Undoubtedly MPLA networks have reappeared here and there in Luanda, in Lobito and its industrial zone, but towns as important as Nova Lisboa and Malange apparently have, for various reasons, only insignificant clandestine activity," he wrote.

The first indication that the FNLA had begun to recruit, or send members into Luanda's slum areas, was in July 1974, following the attacks on the African population by white settlers. Portuguese military and government officials, according to the July 27 *New York Times*, "said agitators of the 'racist' National Front [FNLA] were hiding out in the shantytowns, secure in the knowledge that it would be virtually impossible for the armed forces to find them there. A military spokesman said that large numbers of National Front agents had infiltrated Angola from their bases in neighboring Zaire. . . . some of the National Front's men have apparently slipped through the lines to Luanda and have begun a campaign to win Angolans away from the People's Movement [MPLA], which enjoys wide support here among blacks and whites."

The first public sign of the FNLA's presence was when its flags and banners, along with those of the MPLA, appeared at the funeral held for the Africans who had been killed in the July clashes.

The UNITA, despite its proclaimed strategy of surrounding the towns through rural warfare, also took advantage of the new opportunities. The October 6, 1974, *New York Times* noted that the UNITA "has moved its key men into urban areas to build support among the Angolan Africans."

Pressure continued to mount against Portuguese rule, forcing the MFA to backtrack even further. On July 27, 1974, Spínola said: "the moment has come for the President of the Republic to proclaim, once again and solemnly, the recognition of the right of the peoples of the Portuguese overseas territories to self-determination, including the immediate recognition of their right to independence." But Spínola's "immediate recognition" applied only to the Africans' *right* to independence. It did not mean immediate *independence*. Instead, on August 9, the Portuguese military junta announced a *timetable* for Angola's independence, in which Lisbon declared its intention of remaining in Angola for at least two more years. It also included a proposal for the formation of a coalition government composed of representatives of the three liberation movements and of the "most representative ethnic groups in Angola, including the white population."

In their efforts to bolster the Spínola regime and maintain illusions in its "decolonizing" intentions, the Portuguese Communist and Socialist parties again threw their backing behind this new neocolonial scheme. The July 29, 1974, *Avante*, the daily paper of the Portuguese Communist Party, characterized Spínola's maneuver as a "historic decision that marks the irreversible drive toward the end of the colonial war." At a rally the day before in Evora, Portugal, CP leader Alvaro Cunhal declared, "The Communist party appeals to you, to the whole people, that in the coming days you demonstrate your support in all possible forms to the president of the republic for the decision that has been proclaimed." On July 29, the Communist and Socialist parties assembled 20,000 persons outside the presidential palace to "thank" Spínola for recognizing the colonies' right to independence.

But even the support of the Portuguese Stalinists and Social Democrats could not keep Spínola's schemes from falling apart in his hands. By September his "decolonization" proposals had been greatly eroded: on September 10, Guinea-Bissau won its formal independence; three days earlier, a coalition regime of the Portuguese authorities and Frelimo was set up in Mozambique, with a pledge to grant independence on June 25, 1975.

To stifle the mass mobilizations within Portugal, and to strengthen his hand to push through his schemes in the colonies, Spínola attempted to stage a rightist coup on September 28, 1974. But his previous failures to impose his "solution" on Angola or Mozambique, or to halt the unrest in Portugal, left him isolated within the MFA, and his plot quickly failed. Within two days the colonialist-turned-"decolonizer" was out of power.

The new Lisbon regime, headed by General Costa Gomes, decided to adopt a different neocolonial variant. Rather than attempting to bypass the MPLA, FNLA, and UNITA, it sought to bring them into the Angolan administration in order to use them as political brakes against the rising unrest in the cities. Realizing that the MFA had finally decided to deal directly with the main nationalist groups, the MPLA signed a formal cease-fire agreement on October 1, 1974, and the FNLA did the same a week later. The UNITA had signed a cease-fire agreement in June 1974, although it had continued to oppose Spínola's schemes.

All three groups were allowed to open offices in Luanda. The demonstrations welcoming the MPLA's delegation reflected the extent of that group's support within Luanda, which is predominantly Mbundu, although migrant workers from other parts of the country also lived there at that time. The MPLA representatives were met at the airport November 8 by crowds estimated to number between 30,000 and 50,000 persons. The FNLA delegation, arriving October 30, was greeted by between 4,000 and 5,000 supporters and the UNITA on November 10 by about 20,000 persons.

Both the MPLA and FNLA indicated their willingness to cooperate with the Portuguese in maintaining order within weeks of their arrival in Luanda. In early November a series of clashes in Luanda's muceques left up to a hundred persons, almost all of them Africans, dead. (Although it is not clear what sparked those clashes, sources within the administration and the nationalist groups indicated that it was the result of a factional struggle within the MPLA.) The Portuguese sealed off some of the muceques and imposed a partial curfew on the city, and troops from both the MPLA and FNLA agreed to participate in joint patrols with Portuguese forces to police the city.

Around this time, internal differences within the MPLA surfaced and further complicated the rivalries within the nationalist movement. By mid-1974, at least two factions opposed to the leadership of Agostinho Neto had appeared in the MPLA. One, called the Eastern Revolt, was led by Daniel Chipenda, the Ovimbundu military commander of the MPLA for eastern Angola, who was based in Zambia. In an interview published in the August 22, 1974, *O Provincia de Angola*, Chipenda denounced the "presidentialism" of Neto and called for the unity of the MPLA and FNLA. He also said he favored a "multiracial" Angola in which whites would have full citizenship rights if they obeyed the law. His opposition was particularly significant since he was the most prominent Ovimbundu leader of the MPLA's military forces.

The other group, led by the Reverend Joaquim Pintó de Andrade and called the Active Revolt, was composed of seventy well-known intellectuals and past and present leaders of the MPLA, including Mário Pintó de Andrade, Jaoquim's brother; the Reverend Domingos da Silva, a vice-president of the MPLA; Eduardo Santos and Hugo Menezes, both founding members of the MPLA; and Floribert Monimamba, the chief of operations for the northern front.

In a document drawn up by the group on May 11, 1974, the Active Revolt also attacked the "presidentialism" of the Neto leadership, raised charges of "tribalism and regionalism" in the MPLA's functioning, and criticized the formation of the Supreme Liberation Council with the FNLA in December 1972. In June, Joaquim Pintó de Andrade rejected the idea of negotiations between the MPLA and FNLA. The differences between the Active Revolt and Neto apparently also involved the MPLA's policy toward some of the most important imperialist interests operating in Angola. Jean de la Gueriviève described this aspect of the dispute in the May 31, 1974, *Le Monde*:

Another complaint of the opponents of Mr. Neto concerns the question of oil. A "declaration on oil policy in Angola," published last

February 12 in Dar es Salaam by an aide of Mr. Neto on behalf of the MPLA's executive committee, affirmed that "with the inevitable independence of Angola," all oil companies "that operate on the land and sea will be expelled and their equipment and supplies seized."

This declaration was aimed at the affiliates of Texaco, Petrofina, the Compagnie Française des Pétroles and various Portuguese companies, but above all at Gulf, which has a monopoly on the exploitation of the largest offshore deposits recently discovered off the Cabinda enclave. . . . Afterwards, Mr. Neto had a meeting in Canada with the heads of Gulf.

The adversaries of the president of the MPLA, who affirmed that they had not yet made a decision on the question of oil policy, accused him of acting on his own in his meetings with the Gulf officials.

Neto denounced his opponents within the MPLA by using his standard epithets of "racists" and "tribalists."

At an MPLA congress in Lusaka in August 1974 the Neto faction walked out and Chipenda was elected president. The heads of state of Zambia, the Republic of the Congo, Zaïre, and Tanzania intervened in an effort to get the factions to unify. At a meeting in Brazzaville on September 13, Neto was named president, with Chipenda and Joaquim Pintó de Andrade as vice-presidents. But the "unity" did not last long. Chipenda moved his headquarters to Kinshasa, Zaïre, and on October 29 denounced the cease-fire agreements that had been signed between the three groups and the Portuguese. He claimed that he would continue to fight against Portuguese rule. On November 9, both the FNLA and the Chipenda faction threatened to renew the war if Lisbon recognized the Neto faction, which had set up offices in Luanda the day before.

The Lisbon authorities decided to intervene in the MPLA's internal dispute and tip the balance in favor of Neto's faction and against those of Chipenda and Andrade. According to a report in the December 6, 1974, *Portuguese Africa,* Admiral Rosa Coutinho, a leader of the MFA and high commissioner for Angola, said at a news conference that the MPLA was represented only by the Neto leadership. Coutinho also publicly expressed a preference for the MPLA as more "progressive" than the FNLA and UNITA.

Shortly after, the MPLA announced Chipenda's expulsion, charging him with having been involved in "assassination plots" against Neto in 1972 and 1973 and denouncing his faction's opening of an office in Luanda. While it is not entirely clear, it appears that Chipenda took most of his estimated 2,000 supporters with him. The February 14, 1975, *O Sécula* reported that Neto said he was trying to "reintegrate" the members of the Active Revolt.

With the "resolving" of the MPLA's internal differences, the three liberation movements sat down together and formulated a joint negotiating position to present to the Portuguese.

Under pressure from the Organization of African Unity, which for years had called for the "unification" of the Angolan rivals, a formal unity agreement was signed by all three groups in Mombasa, Kenya, on January 5. The agreement included a "declaration of principles," which stated that Cabinda would remain an integral part of Angola. The three organizations pledged to build a "just and democratic society, rejecting ethnic, racial, and religious discrimination, as well as all other forms of discrimination."

A few days later Roberto noted that the three groups had only agreed to "a common platform for negotiations with Portugal." Each group would maintain its own identity, he said, and during elections "the Angolan people will choose which of them will lead the country." The Angolan peoples, however, never got an opportunity to make such a choice.

From Coalition to Civil War

After less than a week of negotiations in Alvor, Portugal, the FNLA, MPLA, UNITA, and the Lisbon authorities signed accords January 15, 1975. The Alvor accords marked a new stage in Lisbon's "decolonization" plans. The Portuguese military junta agreed to grant Angola its formal independence—but not until November 11 of that year. During the transitional period, the accords stipulated, the country was to be administered by a coalition government of the three nationalist groups and the Portuguese colonial authorities. At the head of the coalition was a presidential council of three members: Johnny Eduardo Pinock for the FNLA, Lopo do Nascimento for the MPLA, and Jose N'Dele for the Unita. Lisbon appointed a high commissioner, Brig. Gen. Silva Cardoso of the MFA to take control of defense and security and to "arbitrate" any differences among the three council members. The FNLA, MPLA, UNITA, and the Portuguese regime were each granted three posts in the cabinet.

The accords also provided for the formation of an "Angolan national army," in which each liberation movement was to have 8,000 troops, while the Portuguese maintained 24,000 troops. A ten-member National Defense Council, headed by General Cardoso, was established with representatives of the three groups and of the Portuguese army, navy, and air force. The nationalist troops were to be integrated into the new army gradually, depending on the "climate of confidence." In an attempt to temporarily freeze the military positions of the MPLA, FNLA, and UNITA, those rebel troops not absorbed into the new army were to remain in the areas they already controlled.

By signing the accords, all three nationalist groups agreed to the continued presence of Portuguese troops in Angola; these troops were allowed to stay until the proclamation of formal independence, when they were to begin withdrawing. According to the agreement, all Portuguese forces were not scheduled to be out of the country until February 29, 1976. The nationalists also compromised on the question of elections. During the negotiations they had pressed for elections following the departure of the Portuguese troops, but the accords provided for the election of a constituent assembly *before* Angola gained its independence and while the Portuguese troops were still in the country. Lisbon intended for the constituent assembly to draw up a new constitution and choose Angola's head of state—with troops in the background to ensure that the constitution reflected Portuguese interests and that the right person ran the country.

The MFA also forced the nationalists to accept other compromises designed to protect Portuguese imperialism's particular economic stake in Angola. Point 54 of the accords stated: "The FNLA, MPLA, and UNITA undertake to respect the property and legitimate interests of Portuguese domiciled in Angola." And while Point 55 did not specifically mention the Portuguese imperialist interests, it did state: "The Portuguese Government on the one hand, and the Liberation Movements on the other, agree to establish between Angola and Portugal constructive and lasting ties of cooperation in all fields, namely technical, cultural, scientific, economic, commercial, monetary, financial and military, on a basis of independence, equality, freedom, mutual respect and reciprocity of interests" (*Portuguese Africa*, January 17, 1975, text reproduced in *Facts and Reports*, February 8, 1975).

The agreement on the coalition regime, by legitimizing the presence of the colonial army, gave the Portuguese imperialists a strong hand in influencing the eventual transition to formal independence. It gave the MFA the opportunity to use the participation of the major nationalist forces in the regime to help control and dampen any mass struggles that arose, to test the strengths and weaknesses of the three groups, and to determine their relative willingness and reliability in administering an "independent" Angola within the capitalist system. It also gave the MFA the chance to try to heighten the existing rivalries among the groups in order to weaken all three.

The MFA delayed the granting of formal independence chiefly to gain time to protect its own interests. But the delay also helped set the stage for all the other imperialist powers to intervene and jockey for position. In January 1975 the White House decided to renew its options with Roberto by authorizing the CIA to "reactivate" its flow of aid. With the $300,000 allocation to the FNLA, Washington hoped to gain leverage with which to influence the "decolonization" process. A few months later $300,000 was also sent to the UNITA.

By accepting posts in the Portuguese-dominated regime, and by agreeing to a prolonged timetable for the transition to formal independence, the three nationalist organizations dangerously compromised the independence struggle and fostered illusions about the MFA among the Angolan and Portuguese masses. Their participation in the coalition regime also revealed the limits of their approach to the struggle for national independence. Rather than forge a united front to mobilize the Angolan peasants and workers to rid the country of Portuguese and other imperialist domination, they chose to collaborate with imperialism—in this case Portuguese imperialism—to achieve their goals. This dangerous error was to be repeated and deepened later on as the factional rivalries among the three groups escalated into a full-scale civil war.

The MFA's decision to deal directly with the three Black nationalist groups, and to exclude white settler representation, was a defeat for the right-wing and openly neocolonialist forces in Angola. But the MFA's recognition of the three groups as the only "legitimate" representatives of the Angolan peoples was an antidemocratic measure that sought to block the development of any other political currents. Point 41 of the accords stated that the only candidates that were to run in the projected elections to the constituent assembly were those of the FNLA, MPLA, and UNITA.

Although Lisbon had not abandoned the Portuguese settlers in Angola, its rejection of their demand for a role in the coalition regime served as a warning to them not to try any adventurist bids to seize control, as the whites in Mozambique had attempted in September 1974, just before the establishment there of a coalition regime that included Frelimo. The white attacks on Luanda's muceques in July and August 1974 had unleashed a response by the Africans that the MFA did not want to see repeated.

Labor Discipline and Investment Guarantees

One of the first tasks the Portuguese authorities sought to carry out with the aid of the coalition regime was to halt the strike wave.

The March 1975 issue of the London monthly *Africa*, after describing the Angolan economy's difficulties, noted that the economic problems had been "exacerbated by a breakdown in labour discipline. For instance, it is estimated that in the ports of Luanda, Lobito and Mocamedes there are about 60 ships waiting to be handled; the stevedores have been striking for better wages or, as one labour leader said, 'to accelerate independence.' The Benguela Railway . . . has also been similarly affected. The cumulative effect of all these problems has been to threaten the seven per cent real growth target that is envisaged for 1975."

Gilbert Comte, in the May 14, 1975, *Le Monde*, reported: "After a long subservience to their employers, the workers are discovering the right to strike. Twenty-five ships paralyzed in the port of Luanda alone, and the unfinished skeletons of about a hundred buildings on which work has been interrupted since April 25 [1974], testify to the fact that they are making use of it. . . ."

Following the nationalization of all Portuguese-owned banks and insurance companies after the defeat of Spínola's second coup attempt on March 11, 1975, which also affected the Angolan branches of those banks, the bank workers' union in Luanda called an assembly to vote on demands for the transfer of the assets of the nationalized Angolan banks to the Angolan government and for a voice in choosing the new bank administrators.

The strikes were not limited to the main port cities. In December 1974 dock workers walked off their jobs in Cabinda, demanding the same wages the Luanda dockers had won through their strike actions. The unrest even affected the South African-financed Cunene hydroelectric dam project in southern Angola near the border with Namibia. The November 1975 issue of *African Development* reported that "there was considerable labour unrest in the immediate aftermath of the Portuguese coup at Calueque [one of the Cunene construction sites], with meetings held by UNITA and the FNLA. In March this year there was a week-long strike over a pay dispute."

Although supporters of all three nationalist groups were apparently participating in the strike wave, the cooperation of the MPLA, FNLA, and UNITA was crucial to Portugal's success in stifling the workers' unrest. All three groups claimed to represent the interests of the Angolan masses, including the workers, but their actions during the first months of the coalition regime revealed their real anti-working class policies.

On February 3, a few days after the installation of the coalition regime, the Presidential Council, on which all three nationalist groups were represented, appealed to "workers and trade union organizations to suspend all their strikes until the necessary regulations and measures safeguarding the rights of the working class are passed and adopted by the Transitional Government." Shortly after, the coalition regime passed a decree that, according to the February 28 *Portuguese Africa*, "allows the government to mobilize workers and place them under military control, discipline and jurisdiction." The decree was then used to break the dockers' strikes at Lobito and Luanda.

According to the June 27 *Angola Report*, Artur Dembo, the UNITA's minister of labor in the coalition regime, "issued an order making unofficial or wildcat strikes illegal, with workers on strike without union backing not being entitled to draw pay. Strikes must have union backing, and must be preceded by negotiation."

The nationalist leaders also made personal efforts to persuade workers to stop their strikes. The June 1975 *Africa* reported: "In January this year, Jonas Savimbi, the UNITA leader, appealed to strikers at the docks [of Lobito] to return to work. Pointing to a Zambian journalist, he said to the dockers, 'Do you think that the people of his country can do without these goods? They are in the front line of the liberation struggle.' His words settled this dispute and traffic to Zambia flowed once again."

At a news conference in Angola in February, MPLA leader Agostinho Neto appealed to all Angola workers "to apply themselves more to their work, because now, more than ever, it is necessary to work to help the reconstruction of the country." He then added, "Striking is the defense of the worker and the worker has the right to defend himself, to show that he is against exploitation, of which he is, in most cases, a victim." Neto continued, "It is, however, necessary that strikes are duly organized through the proper organs, in this case the unions, and not by just anybody without qualifications for this."

In some areas the factional rivalry among the nationalist groups appears to have been a factor in the strikebreaking campaign. The Lisbon *Diário de Notícias*, which at the time generally favored the MPLA in its news coverage, reported in the February 28 issue that "the MPLA accused UNITA of being responsible for the strike that paralyzed the harbor of Lobito. In an MPLA declaration issued in Lobito, Savimbi's movement is being accused of provoking tribal and regional disturbances. MPLA troops occupied the harbor and tried to make the workers change their minds. These workers were mostly Bailundos [Ovimbundus], on whom the MPLA has little influence. According to press reports UNITA then sent a military unit to the waterfront, whereupon the MPLA forces withdrew."

Despite the repressive measures, Luanda dock workers again walked off their jobs on May 28. A few days earlier, dockers with five and ten years' seniority were granted 15 and 30 percent wage increases respectively. Those with less than five years' seniority then demanded equal rates of pay. The May 30 *Angola Report*, a Luanda news service, reported, "The dockers union, SINTAPA, said the strike was unofficial and did not have the union's support, and called on the Government to take adequate measures." The strikers, however, were steadfast. "The strike in the port of Luanda continues," said the June 6 *Angola Report*, "despite appeals by the dockers union, SINTAPA, for the men to go back to work and despite personal visits by ministers and senior officials who talked to the strikers. The authorities say they have paid the men everything that had been agreed on; no new claims have been presented."

On March 8 a demonstration was held in front of the government building in Luanda to protest the law placing workers at ports and in other key industries under military discipline. Although the MPLA reportedly had considerable political influence on the groups (called "people's committees") that organized it, the demonstration was not linked to the MPLA. In fact, Lopo do Nascimento, the MPLA member on the Presidential Council, even tried to defend the law, saying it was "not against the interests of the people."

After proving their willingness to discipline the workers, all three nationalist groups went on to show that they were equally willing to protect foreign investments. In fact, they made special efforts to reassure the imperialists that further investments were welcome.

The MPLA, in particular, faced an obstacle in convincing foreign investors that their capital was safe in its hands: it had to make them understand that its socialist and anti-imperialist rhetoric was only for appearances. A radio broadcast from Luanda on November 14, 1974, less than a week after the MPLA set up offices in the capital, reported: "A delegation of the MPLA met yesterday with about three dozen members of economic organizations of Angola and the commercial bank to exchange ideas and to clarify positions about Angola's future economy. The MPLA representative declared that to call MPLA a communist party is nonsense, 'as well as accusations that we are racialists,'" (as cited in *Facts and Reports*, December 21, 1974).

Less than two weeks after the Lisbon coup, Neto also tried to reassure the Portuguese settlers in Angola: "After independence, the Portuguese living in Africa can remain. . . . They will not lose their economic interests and there will be no violence. If the Portuguese are afraid, it is because of the tendentious propaganda against us and perhaps also because we have not sufficiently defined our objectives for after the war" (*Le Monde*, May 5-6, 1974).

In an interview in the April 6 *Sunday News* of Tanzania, Lopo do Nascimento of the MPLA was asked: "Is it the intention of your Movement to nationalise these [foreign economic] interests, or to hand them over to individual Angolans?" Nascimento replied: "We call for state participation in companies which are exploiting our country's resources. We uphold the principle of development which makes it possible to transform our country's resources in such a way that there really is economic development which benefits Angolans. . . . The nationalisation of enterprises is a fairly complex problem which implies having national cadres and sound knowledge of new techniques, so as to ensure that such enterprises will continue to operate properly after nationalisation. So we have set aside this possibility for now."

UNITA's Jonas Savimbi, who describes himself as a "moderate, nondogmatic socialist" and who claims that the UNITA is "anticapitalist," explained in an interview published in the February 22, 1975, issue of the British magazine *To the Point International* that "we want good relations with the West and particularly with the EEC [European Economic Community]. We already have contact with some EEC countries and want to deepen these relations because we think Europe will play a moderating role in the international situation. . . . We must have free enterprise. If we took away the stimulus of profit then we would have stagnation . . . I think we should follow the example of that great African statesman, President Houphouet Boigny of the Ivory Coast." In another interview, Savimbi said he would favor a state that would "leave as much as possible of the economy to private enterprise." He stated that "we welcome any source of foreign investment, and will give the investor all facilities and guarantees" (*Portuguese Africa*, April 28, 1975).

One of the EEC countries that the UNITA made special overtures toward was France. According to the July 14, 1975, Lisbon daily *O Século*, UNITA official John Kakumba Marques "stated at a press conference in Dakar that he was in favor of cooperation with France. He viewed as 'positive' the statement of the French Minister of Cooperation, Pierre Abelin, according to whom the doors of cooperation are open between France and the former Portuguese colonies."

Jeremias Chitunda, the UNITA minister of natural resources in the coalition regime, had told a news conference in Luanda March 3 that the dominant position of South African companies in Angola's mining industry was not in the best interests of the Angolan population, but added, "I do not want to talk about nationalizing private companies at this time."

The FNLA has made few statements on its economic policy. However, in a July 3, 1975, speech at a conference on African development planning in Tunis, FNLA leader Holden Roberto outlined his movement's position. Although he claimed to be for "socialism with a human face," the July 5 *Zambia Daily Mail* reported that according to Roberto the FNLA "would respect private property, private initiative and basic freedoms, while operating an economic system geared to a largely 'self-managing' development involving the entire Angolan people. The state would play a leading role in this 'self-management' system of socialism by making sure economic production was kept to a maximum and wealth was shared in 'the most fair' way, he said."

Despite the factional differences between the MPLA, FNLA, and UNITA, they had no trouble in agreeing on the basic points of a common economic program. In fact, neither did Vasco Vieira de Almeida, the Portuguese economic affairs minister in the coalition regime. Almeida was the one who wrote it. The program, according to a summary in the June 13 *Marchés Tropicaux*, called for the "rapid elimination of foreign capital from those sectors vital to national activity. However, foreign capital will not be excluded from participating in the development of the country." The program also pledged to "safeguard the legitimate interests of private initiative" and called for state control of 51 percent of the oil, natural gas, diamond, uranium, iron, wolfram, gold, and copper industries.

Such measures are no different from those enacted in many

other formally independent African states which are still economically subordinate to the imperialist powers.

To ensure a privileged position for Lisbon in the continued exploitation of Angola's vast natural wealth, Almeida included in the program a point calling for "reinforcement" of the economic relations between Angola and Portugal.

However, there was one much-needed economic reform that the MPLA, FNLA, and UNITA pledged to carry out: the expropriation of the large coffee plantations in northern Angola. According to the May 25, 1975, issue of the Tanzania *Sunday News*, Saydi Mingas, the MPLA's minister of economic planning and finance in the coalition regime, said in a radio interview that many of the big coffee estates in the Carmona and Luanda regions had been developed on land "stolen from the Africans—even from the colonial government. For us, there is no other way to solve the problem—to expropriate all these properties." He then added, "We will have no difficulty in having agreement of all the liberation movements to expropriate these lands from the Portuguese settlers."

One of the coffee plantations—the largest in the world—which was owned by the Portuguese state enterprise Companhia Angola de Agricultura, employed 10,000 workers. About 125,000 Africans were employed altogether on the white-owned estates. The *Sunday News* commented on the proposed expropriation of these estates: "The exploitation of labour by the Portuguese plantocracy, with their armed foremen and guard dogs, cannot continue under independence, however moderate the incoming government."

Preparing for the Showdown

Although Roberto, Neto, and Savimbi agreed that capitalism was to be maintained in an "independent" Angola, each had his own idea of who should administer the country. With the prospect of the Portuguese withdrawal not far off, the factional rivalries that had developed over the years—reinforced by the different ethnic bases of the three groups—came to the fore. Even before they entered the coalition government, the MPLA, FNLA, and UNITA moved to consolidate and expand their own organizations as rapidly as possible.

In December 1974, the Aliança das Populações de Angola (APA—Angolan Peoples' Alliance) merged with the FNLA. On

April 17, 1975, Roberto also accepted into membership former MPLA leader Daniel Chipenda and his estimated 2,000 troops. Chipenda was placed on the FNLA's National Council of the Revolution and on its Political Bureau. He was also named assistant secretary-general.

In the May 15, 1975, *Le Monde*, Gilbert Comte described the FNLA's recruitment efforts in the north: "Since November, emissaries have traveled through the villages, selecting youths to carry weapons. Each day, trucks filled with recruits leave Carmona for the distant camps of Kinkusu and Kotacoli, in Zaïre." The FNLA also reinforced its military position in Luanda and sent 500 troops to the port city of Lobito in central Angola. By the end of April, 300,000 refugees had returned to Angola. Many of them were Bakongos who had been living in exile; thus part of the FNLA's base of support shifted back into the country.

The MPLA's dominant position in Luanda was demonstrated February 4 when it held a rally of hundreds of thousands to commemorate the anniversary of the outbreak of armed actions in Luanda in 1961. This broad support helped it attract a number of other nationalist groups in the Luanda region. After the signing of the Alvor accords, the executive of the Angola Democratic Socialist Front (Fresda—Frente Socialista Democrática de Angola) dissolved the organization and called on its members to join the MPLA. The Angola Democratic Movement (MDA—Movimento Democrático de Angola) also merged with the MPLA. The African National League (LNA—Liga Nacional Africana), while maintaining its own organization, gave its general support to the MPLA. The LNA had originally been formed in the 1930s as a government-sponsored organization, in a Portuguese attempt to directly control some of the nationalist currents in Angola. After the Lisbon coup, the LNA's Portuguese-backed leaders had been ousted.

The Organization of African Unity did not officially recognize the UNITA es a liberation movement up to the time of the Lisbon coup, but in October 1974 it extended de facto recognition by giving it some OAU funds (as it had to the MPLA and FNLA earlier).

Some former MPLA members who had left with Chipenda joined the UNITA rather than follow him into the FNLA. Marcos Kassanga, who had been the UPA's chief of staff until he left it in 1962, also joined the UNITA (*A Província de Angola*, March 19, 1975).

Although the UNITA steadily increased its support among the Ovimbundu of the central plateau, it remained the weakest of the three groups militarily through early 1975. As a consequence it tried to maintain the appearance of being aloof from the factional struggle and stressed the theme of unity among the three groups. Before the signing of the unity agreement in Mombasa, Kenya, in early January, Savimbi acted as a moderator between the MPLA and FNLA.

The UNITA's policy of pushing for unity was also extended to the white settlers in the country. After the accords with Lisbon were signed in January, UNITA spokesman Jorge Valentim stated, "Everyone in Angola will be Angolan." The settlers' "headaches are finished," he said. Such assurances won the UNITA some support among the settler population, although whites reportedly joined all three groups. According to Colin Legum, writing in the January-February 1975 *Problems of Communism*, Fernando Falção, the leader of the neocolonialist FUA, made overtures to the UNITA, but the idea of any alliance between them was publicly repudiated by Savimbi.

While the leaders of the three groups continued to participate in the coalition regime, and launched joint attacks against striking workers, their troops began to fight each other in the streets of Luanda.

The first major clashes after the installation of the coalition regime were between the MPLA forces of Agostinho Neto and troops of Daniel Chipenda's grouping. The clashes followed the MPLA's refusal to recognize the right of any group other than the MPLA, FNLA, and UNITA to exist and function. On February 14, the MPLA released a statement trying to justify this position. "Our organizations were recognized as the only negotiators with the Portuguese Government, whose cooperation made the decolonization process possible," the MPLA said. "All organizations and military forces not integrated in the liberation movements thus were considered illegal, and therefore subject to disbanding." This MPLA interpretation of the Alvor accords was inaccurate. While the accords barred any group other than the three main ones from participating in the regime or running in the elections, they were not specifically made illegal. The official MPLA leadership had already asked Chipenda in January to disband his forces. The January 31 *República* reported that Chipenda had attempted to enter the eastern city of Luso with an armed force, but was halted by MPLA troops, who were supported by Portuguese forces. The ruling Armed Forces Movement (MFA) which had earlier backed the Neto faction against Chipenda's, apparently did not want to see a fourth nationalist group established in Angola. Two months after the February clashes in Luanda between the MPLA and Chipenda's forces, Chipenda joined the FNLA, thus obtaining a "legal" status for his troops.

A month after the MPLA-Chipenda confrontations, units of the MPLA and FNLA fought in various parts of the country, particularly in the muceques of Luanda. Heavy fighting again broke out at the end of April and lasted through mid-June. Many civilians were caught in the cross fire. The Luanda morgue announced May 3 that 500 bodies had been brought in; but since many of the dead had not yet been picked up, the toll may have reached as high as 1,000.

In a show of strength, the MPLA-affiliated trade union, UNTA (União Nacional dos Trabalhadores de Angola—National Union of Angolan Workers) called a general strike in Luanda May 22. It had originally been scheduled for May 1, but was banned at that time by the coalition regime because of the fighting. According to Reuters, the strike was generally successful, with 15,000 persons attending a rally.

The MPLA also attempted to use the "people's committees" and neighborhood commissions that had been formed in Luanda after the July-August 1974 rightist attacks as a factional lever against its rivals. Under the slogan of "people's power," Neto called for the greater participation of these committees in the "resolution of political problems." The May 15, 1975, *Le Monde* reported that the MPLA was distributing arms to youths in the muceques.

The limited role the MPLA assigned to these groups was revealed later. When the FNLA and UNITA had been driven out of the city, and they were no longer needed, the MPLA moved to disarm the committees and bureaucratically impose its own political control over them.

The FNLA, using anti-Communist rhetoric, called for the dissolution of these committees, which generally backed the MPLA. In response to the MPLA's slogan of "people's power," Roberto declared that "people's power leads to a people's dictatorship and the population of Angola, which is Christian, actively rejects Communism" (Agence France-Presse, February 18, 1975). About a month later he stated in a radio broadcast that "within the context of our country, as you know, direct democracy is not possible."

From the beginning of May and into June, the fighting spread to most of the important towns in northern Angola; there were reports of clashes in Santo António do Zaire, Uíge, Ambrizete, Malange, Dalatando, and Carmona. Fighting also took place in the Cabinda enclave, in the central city of Nova Lisboa, and in Teixeira de Sousa on the Benguela railway in eastern Angola. According to a report by David B. Ottaway in the June 10, 1975, *Washington Post*, much of the fighting in the northern part of the country appeared to be the result of MPLA and FNLA efforts to clear pockets of rival troops out of areas that had been under their influence. He said that the FNLA in the Bakongo area "has now pretty well eliminated the presence of Popular Movement troops throughout this region." The MPLA was likewise moving against FNLA forces in the territory north and east of Luanda.

Although the UNITA throughout the first months of the fighting said it was not involved, it was drawn into armed clashes in early June. "In an official statement," the June 8 *Washington Post* reported, "Portugal authorities accused the MPLA of attacking UNITA, but added that the MPLA forces were apparently acting without orders from their high command." The UNITA later issued a statement saying that it had "no quarrel" with the MPLA.

The fighting caused a panic among the Portuguese settlers. Hundreds of thousands began fleeing the plantations of northern Angola and towns and cities throughout the country, converging on Luanda for a mass exodus back to Portugal. The fighting also caused some concern among several of the foreign companies operating in Angola. Because of the clashes in Cabinda, Gulf Oil evacuated the dependents of its employees. But a Gulf official maintained that production at its Malongo facilities twenty miles north of the city of Cabinda was "normal." Texaco likewise evacuated all of its personnel from Santo António do Zaire, close to its offshore exploration facilities, after the town was captured by the FNLA.

The MFA's "Active Neutrality"

Despite its public statements deploring the fighting in Angola, the Armed Forces Movement regime in Lisbon was not necessarily opposed to the fratricidal conflict. It gave the MFA a greater opportunity to play the groups off against each other in its own interests; it weakened the entire Angolan nationalist struggle;

and it provided a cover for the strikebreaking campaign. At the same time, the MFA realized that the growing conflict could potentially endanger Portuguese interests if it got out of control, or if any of the three groups decided to turn against the Portuguese as well. To prevent such a turn of events, the MFA decided to remind the nationalists that Portuguese troops were still in the country and capable of taking action if necessary.

"Faced with the growing danger of civil war in Angola," according to the June 9, 1975, *Los Angeles Times*, "Portugal's Supreme Revolutionary Council reportedly has taken a decision to reinforce its 24,000-strong army in the African colony."

Explaining the MFA's policy of "active neutrality" in Angola, President Costa Gomes said, according to the June 6 *Jornal Novo*, that the Portuguese armed forces "would not hesitate to intervene" in the colony to prevent a "deterioration of the situation."

In Luanda, the MFA ordered its troops to shoot any member of the nationalist groups seen fighting. A spokesman for the Portuguese high command in Luanda said June 9 that Portuguese paratroopers had stormed the strongholds of the MPLA and FNLA and seized their arms stocksm A few weeks before, according to the May 17 South African *Star Weekly*, Portuguese troops intervened ageinst the MPLA and FNLA in Nova Lisboa.

In the interests of its own factional struggle for power, the MPLA made a dangerous error: it urged the Portuguese forces to intervene in the fighting on the MPLA's side. In March the MPLA criticized "the passivity of the Portuguese Armed Forces in Angola, which constitutes a clear violation of the Alvor accords and aids the political destabilization fomented by imperialism." The May 2 *Jornal Novo* reported that Neto released a statement in which he said that the Angolan "people continue to wait for the high commissioner and the Portuguese troops to assume their responsibilities."

The MPLA even gave the MFA a political rationale for armed intervention. Referring to those forces in favor of establishing a "neocolonialist regime" in Angola (i.e., those groups opposed to the MPLA), the MPLA declared in a March statement: "A victory for the imperialist forces in Angola would represent a mortal threat to the future of democracy in Portugal and will imperil peace in all of Africa. The MPLA is the only progressive movement in Angola, the only movement that will support and loyally cooperate with the progressive Portuguese forces."

The MPLA statements gave the Lisbon regime a cover for its continued presence in Angola and politically disoriented those forces in both Angola and Portugal—including the Portuguese troops themselves—that would have been in a position to counter Lisbon's efforts to retain its most important interests in the colony. Even from the MPLA's own limited factional viewpoint, the call for Portuguese intervention was very risky, as the June 9 Portuguese assault against both the FNLA and MPLA showed.

The MFA's military options in the colony were limited, however. Even if the MFA tried to use the subterfuge of intervening in Angola against "neocolonialism," it would have been difficult to move thousands of reinforcements into the colony or use the troops already there in a massive way. If it had tried, the results could have been politically explosive within Portugal's population and especially among the ranks of the army. But the Portuguese troops were still capable of a limited intervention under the guise of "maintaining order."

The MFA government on May 10 called for a meeting with the three main nationalist groups, ostensibly to avert a civil war. The following day, FNLA head Roberto stated: "Given the evident partiality and lack of objectivity shown by certain members of the Government of Lisbon to our movement . . . the FNLA categorically refuses to take part in a meeting of the three Angolan movements with which a member of the Portuguese Government will be associated." UNITA leader Jonas Savimbi also rejected Portuguese participation in such a meeting.

However, Savimbi managed to organize a summit meeting of the three rival nationalist groups which began in Kenya June 15, without the participation of the Portuguese. On June 21, 1975, the three groups agreed publicly to halt the fighting, free prisoners held by each group, disarm civilians, and merge their forces into a "single army."

The Factional Struggle for Power

The June cease-fire agreement was short-lived. Within weeks the skirmishes in Luanda escalated once again into major battles, as the MPLA launched a concerted drive to force its rivals from the city. By mid-July the FNLA's headquarters in Luanda had been destroyed by mortar and artillery bombardment and most of its forces had been pushed out of the capital. A few days later the UNITA started the evacuation of its 5,000 troops garrisoned in Luanda.

Although the FNLA and UNITA officially retained their posts in the coalition government for several more weeks, their withdrawal from Luanda marked a de facto collapse of the coalition set up in January. In fact, it signaled the beginning of a full-scale civil war. After the new clashes the FNLA put its military units throughout the country on a permanent state of alert and ordered its troops to "resist the military coup launched by Lisbon and its agents in Angola." Two weeks later the UNITA ordered the mobilization of its forces.

With the expulsion of the FNLA and UNITA from Luanda, the MPLA had secured its dominance of the city. This MPLA victory, however, sparked an exodus of the Bakongo and Ovimbundu supporters of the FNLA and UNITA, who apparently feared reprisals from the predominantly Mbundu supporters of the MPLA.

This process actually began during the fighting that swept the city several weeks earlier. The June 12, 1975, Lisbon *Diário de Notícias* reported: "Before the Government palace in Luanda hundreds of African workers were demonstrating, demanding transportation to leave Luanda. These workers, mainly belonging to UNITA, consider themselves unsafe in the Angolan capital.

UNITA leaders with megaphones tried to calm down the demonstrators." The July 28 issue of *Jornal de Angola*, which by that time had come under the control of the MPLA, reported, "Thousands of Angolans from Uíge and Zaire provinces [Bakongo areas] are flocking together on the square in front of the palace and demanding transportation to the areas they come from."

The MPLA followed up its victory in Luanda by taking control of several other important cities along the coast, including Lobito, Benguela, Moçâmedes, and Sá da Bandeira. In late October and early November, however, the MPLA retreated from these cities in the face of an armored column composed of rival nationalist troops backed up by white mercenaries and South African regulars.

The real victims of the Angolan civil war were the African masses in both the urban and rural areas. By August, the Red Cross estimated, more than half a million Africans had been displaced by the fighting; this figure climbed even higher in the months that followed. The death toll was heavy. According to the August 8 *Angola Report*, published in Luanda, refugees arriving in Nova Lisboa said that "bodies are lying rotting in the streets of Malange, and that the water supply there has been contaminated. Gabela is a ghost town. . . ."

The northern part of Angola, the traditional base of the FNLA, was particularly hard hit. The August 1 *Angola Report* said, "Really serious is the plight of many of the Angolans who took refuge in neighbouring Zaire at the start of the war [in 1961]. Their number is estimated at about 2/3 of a million, and nearly 500,000 of them have returned. . . . the Bishop of Carmona last week told visiting correspondents that between 40 and 50 were dying of starvation every day."

The hunger in the northern areas continued into 1976, and apparently became a factor in the war between the MPLA and FNLA. *New York Times* correspondent Michael T. Kaufman reported in the January 7, 1976, issue that the International Committee of the Red Cross said "there was great hardship and near starvation in some sections, notably the northern Bakongo lands near the border with Zaire." The United Nations High Commission for Refugees, which had asked the MPLA for permission to fly relief supplies to the Bakongo areas, was expelled from Luanda by the MPLA after Angola officially gained its independence November 11.

The MFA did not sit by idly while the civil war escalated. It continued to practice its policy of "active neutrality." The Portuguese military junta's Revolutionary Council held an emergency session July 14 as the fighting flared, and later announced that it had discussed reinforcing its army of 24,000 troops still stationed in the colony. The next day a Portuguese military representative in Luanda said that two planeloads of troops had arrived from Portugal. On his way to Angola, the foreign minister, Maj. Ernesto Melo Antunes, said that Portuguese troops might have to intervene in the fighting to prevent "massacres."

A week later he specified whom this declaration was directed against. According to the July 21 *O Século*, "Minister Melo Antunes asserted that in order to prevent a massacre of the civilian population, the Portuguese government has decided to block the military reconquest of Luanda by the Frente Nacional de Libertação de Angola." Antunes's concern for "civilians" was apparently for the Portuguese settlers, who had converged on Luanda for their exodus back to Portugal; the Lisbon military officers were not known for their interest in safeguarding Africans.

A dispatch from Luanda published in the July 22 *Diário de Notícias* reported: "A Portuguese military spokesman declared in this city yesterday that troops belonging to one of the African nationalist movements involved in the fighting in the Angolan capital had begun to infiltrate along the coast yesterday in the direction of Luanda. However, he added that Portuguese forces would intervene to intercept these troops, belonging to the Frente Nacional de Libertação de Angola (FNLA), and prevent them from entering the city."

And a military source in Lisbon offered this hypocritical justification for Portuguese actions against the FNLA: "We just can't let the Front violate cease-fire agreements and take advantage of our desire to free the colony" (*Washington Post*, July 27, 1975).

The day after Antunes made his declaration, the FNLA announced that "the Lisbon government has declared war on the FNLA." The FNLA then called for "a general offensive against the Portuguese neocolonialists and the agents of social-imperialism." In the lingo of the FNLA, the latter term was a reference to the MPLA.

The FNLA forces did not get close enough to Luanda to test the seriousness of the MFA's threats. But on July 27, a Portuguese military unit attacked a group of MPLA members and bystanders in Luanda, killing twenty. The Portuguese troops claimed they were attempting to arrest MPLA troops who had shot several Portuguese soldiers earlier. After the attack, Neto called for the immediate withdrawal of all Portuguese troops from Angola. Neto's declaration, however, did not mean an end to the MPLA's collaboration with the colonial authorities. He stated at the time that he still considered the Portuguese regime an ally of the liberation movements (*Manchester Guardian Weekly*, August 2, 1975).

On August 14, Gen. Ernesto Fereira do Macedo, the acting Portuguese high commissioner in Angola, announced the dissolution of the coalition regime and took over all executive powers, including the authority to declare a state of siege and suspend constitutional rights. On August 29 the MFA scrapped the Alvor accords, which had pledged Lisbon to turn over power to the three nationalist groups on November 11.

The MPLA's initial response to this move was to declare, "We, the MPLA, reaffirm once again to the Portuguese Government that the Angolan people will not abandon their rights and will not hesitate to defend them by force of arms." On September 15, Neto repeated his call for the withdrawal of Portuguese troops from Angola by November 11. The UNITA's assistant secretary-general John Kakumba Marques, declared in Kinshasa September 3 that the UNITA did not recognize the authority of the Portuguese high commissioner, and he demanded that Lisbon "immediately withdraw its forces from Angola." The FNLA ran a front-page editorial in the September 15 issue of *Independence Totale*, its weekly English-language bulletin, entitled: "FNLA Demands Immediate Withdrawal of Portuguese Forces From Angola."

Lisbon also faced growing opposition to its continued presence in Angola from the Portuguese troops themselves. On September 1 about 200 troops, the majority from the military police regiment, joined a demonstration of 5,000 persons in Lisbon demanding that no more soldiers be sent to Angola and that the troops already there be brought home. Following the protest, several companies of military police refused orders to go to Angola. The MFA was worried by these protests. During a September 10 television broadcast in Portugal, delegates of the MFA from Angola described the problems facing the colonial army; the most important, in their view, was the refusal of troops to go to Angola. One MFA delegate denounced the "opportunism and cowardice" of the protesting soldiers.

While the Lisbon protests involved only a few hundred, they were symptomatic of the widespread discontent within the ranks of the army, including the troops in Angola. A report by correspondent Filipe Vieira in the September 30 *Jornal Novo* described the low morale of the Portuguese troops in Nova Lisboa, in central Angola. Noting that they were "completely demobilized psychologically," he said: "The action of the Military Police contingents in Lisbon, who were assigned to patrol the city [Nova Lisboa] but who refused to go to Angola, will intensify the feeling of isolation among the troops even more.

"To leave, to get out of Nova Lisboa, is already a universal thought, a fixed idea argued calendar in hand."

The unreliability of the Portuguese troops, and the political opposition of the MPLA, FNLA, and UNITA to their continued presence in the country, were major factors in the MFA's decision to pull out of Angola by November 11. The new Portuguese high commissioner, Adm. Leonel Cardoso, announced September 18 that most combat troops would be withdrawn by that date. Cardoso tried to suggest that paternalistic considerations were behind this move; according to a dispatch in the September 20 *Diário de Notícias*, "the high commissioner said the withdrawal reflected the confidence that Portugal has in the good people of this vast territory."

Although the MPLA had at first denounced the suspension of the Alvor accords and the dissolution of the four-way coalition regime, it soon realized that those moves had been to its factional benefit. The order dissolving the coalition provided for the Portuguese take-over of only those ministries that had been "abandoned" by the FNLA and UNITA. The posts were actually being filled by MPLA officials, although the arrangement was an informal one. This allowed the MPLA to extend its control over the Luanda administration while the Portuguese were still in formal authority. "Even Portuguese who do not like the MPLA's leftist leanings admit that the MPLA is establishing disciplined control in Luanda," Dial Torgerson reported in the September 13 *Los Angeles Times*. "Its police are replacing Portuguese police who were among the first to fly to Lisbon."

In an interview published in the October 24, 1975, *Marchés Tropicaux*, Neto explained: "The unilateral suspension of the

Alvor accords by Portugal was determined by concrete reasons. The departure of the ministers of the transitional government who had been named by the FNLA and UNITA and the constant violations of the accords by those movements led Portugal to take that position. The MPLA remained in the transitional government and benefited from this situation as a result of the persistence it showed in the defense of the people's interests."

The MPLA was also represented on a coordinating body set up within the National Commission for Decolonization at the time the coalition was dissolved. That body was headed by Portuguese President Costa Gomes and included several other Lisbon officials.

An important wing of the MFA apparently considered the MPLA, of the three groups, the one in a position to be most useful in safeguarding Lisbon's interests in Angola. The most outspoken representative of this wing was Adm. Rosa Coutinho, who served as high commissioner before the establishment of the Luanda coalition regime. It also included Costa Gomes, Cooperation Minister Vitor Crespo, Foreign Minister Melo Antunes, Gen. Carlos Fabião, and Gen. Otelo Saraiva de Carvalho, among others. This attitude by some of the Portuguese officers had been evident as early as November 1974. For instance, the London *Financial Times* had reported from Lisbon November 27: "It is no secret here the armed forces movement finds the MPLA the most ideologically attractive movement although it is at pains to appear the neutral referee."

Crespo, who had served as high commissioner in Mozambique during the period of the coalition regime there, repeated this theme in October 1975, when he said that since the MFA and the Lisbon regime had a political affinity with "the progressive ideas of the MPLA. . .we would naturally like to see the same forces involved in the future politics of Angola" (*Daily News* of Tanzania, October 25, 1975).

Besides the fact that both the MPLA and MFA were adept at using socialist rhetoric to disguise their procapitalist policies, a more important reason that a wing of the MFA decided to back the MPLA was the MPLA's strong political influence on the Luanda workers and the Mbundu people in the Luanda-Malange region. The MPLA was viewed as being in a better position to control workers' struggles in Angola's main industrial center than either of its two rivals. Because it had the adherence of many Angola intellectuals, both African and Portuguese, the

MPLA was also viewed as being more capable of administering the country.

After the Portuguese withdrawal Cardoso, the last high commissioner, declared that "Angola cannot be governed without the MPLA" because it "has the entire administrative machinery in its hands. . . .Without the MPLA, anyone who tried to sit in the chair that I left vacant would fall within eight days, without even being pushed. It is indispensible to me that the MPLA be in any government, either with the MPLA in the lead or with its cooperation" (*Diário de Notícias*, November 24, 1975).

To ensure that this wing of the MFA did not change its mind, Lopo do Nascimento, who had been prime minister in the coalition regime, repeated the MPLA's pledge to protect foreign investments. In an interview in the September 5 *Jornal Novo*, Nascimento said the MPLA still considered valid the economic program drawn up by Vasco Vieira de Almeida, which called for the "reinforcement" of the economic relations between Lisbon and Angola. Nascimento added that the MPLA would not go "too fast" within the framework of that program. "All capitalists face the problem of nationalizations," he said, "but we of the MPLA have nearly direct knowledge of what happened in many other African countries where certain solutions (nationalizations) were taken prematurely and were not the most opportune. Therefore, we have taken these experiences into account and hope to be cautious and act with a certain realism." Nascimento stressed that "there is now no reason for the existing companies to get alarmed."

In addition to allowing the MPLA to extend its control over the Luanda administration, Cardoso made a modest contribution to the MPLA's war chest. Following the September 18 announcement that Lisbon would withdraw most of its troops by November 11, a correspondent of the British Broadcasting Corporation mentioned a report that Portuguese military supplies in Angola would be equally divided between the three liberation movements. The October 5 *Jornal de Angola*, which was controlled by the MPLA, reported the admiral's denial: "I have never said that. . . . We shall transfer everything to the administrative or governmental institutions. The Navy's share will be handed over to the Serviços de Marinha. The ships have been handed over already on October 1. The Aéronautica Civil will receive the things of the Portuguese Air Force, while the Army will transfer some matériel to the Road-building Service, some to the Institute of Industrial Development, etc." (Cited in the October 18 Amsterdam *Facts and Reports*).

With the MPLA in virtually total control of Luanda, where almost all the remaining government bodies were located, this move was a de facto transfer of Portuguese arms to the MPLA. After reporting that Cardoso had reconstituted the Presidential Council in Luanda to give legal status to Nascimento's position in the regime, the October 20 issue of the Nigerian *West Africa* commented, "Since the High Commissioner has announced that all military and other equipment will be bequeathed, not to the guerrilla groups, but to 'organs of the state,' the legitimisation of the MPLA government is crucial to their claim to it."

Cardoso decided, however, not to leave all the Portuguese equipment in Angola. The heavy arms were shipped back to Portugal. According to the November 14 issue of the Paris magazine *Jeune Afrique*, the arms left for the MPLA included ammunition, many thousands of rifles and machine guns, two small planes, and twenty-five coastal patrol boats.

The MPLA called on Lisbon to recognize its regime as the only legitimate government of Angola. It staged demonstrations in Luanda; and the Portuguese Communist Party and a number of small groups on the CP's left flank held actions in Lisbon to pressure the MFA to recognize the MPLA regime. Cardoso, in a "civilian capacity," spoke at one of these rallies, held on October 26, by the MPLA in Luanda.

The policy of the Lisbon military junta as a whole, however, was a more cautious one. A pro-MPLA report in the October 10 Mozambique *Notícias* explained one reason for this caution: "Circles related to the Portuguese Government state that for the moment they have to act with care. They ask for understanding in this matter. Thousands of settlers still are in the areas under the control of the FNLA and UNITA reactionaries, and their lives would seriously be endangered in case the Portuguese Government showed its sympathy and openly supported the MPLA."

A more important reason was the uncertainty of the MPLA's chances of winning the fratricidal war. If Lisbon officially aided the MPLA in its struggle for power, as the MPLA asked it to do, Portuguese interests in Angola could have been jeopardized in the event of an FNLA and UNITA victory. The safest policy, in the view of the Portuguese, was to leave the doors open to cooperation with whatever nationalist force gained dominance. It was for that reason that when the last of the Portuguese troops pulled out of Angola on November 10, the MFA did not formally recognize any of the contending nationalist groups.

Although the country continued to face grave dangers from the imperialist powers, particularly the United States and South Africa, the end of direct Portuguese colonial rule marked a historic victory for the Angolan peoples, a victory that had been paid for by many years of suffering and struggle.

The MPLA's "People's Republic of Angola"

The People's Republic of Angola was not officially proclaimed by the MPLA until November 11, 1975. The MPLA, however, had begun preparations for the installation of the regime as early as August, when the coalition including the FNLA and UNITA was officially dissolved.

From the MPLA's point of view, one of the prerequisites for the consolidation of its control over Luanda was an end to the strike wave that had been going on for more than a year, since the Lisbon coup.

After the ouster of the FNLA and UNITA from Luanda, the MPLA continued to exhort workers to "produce more." One of its slogans was: "Refusing to work is treason against the Angolan people." *Jornal Novo* correspondent José Manuel Teixeira reported from Luanda September 2 that Nito Alves, a member of the MPLA's Political Bureau, made "an appeal to workers to remain at their posts and to suspend their strikes. . . ." Alves also "publicly affirmed that it is an error to say that there is a class struggle in Angola that pits the bourgeoisie against the proletariat."

The dock workers, who had staged some of the most militant strikes, bore the brunt of this campaign. MPLA troops and representatives from the MPLA-dominated neighborhood committees went to the docks to "help" the workers load and unload ships. The workday at Luanda harbor was extended to last until late at night. In a speech in late September, Nascimento accused dockers who did not work of carrying out "sabotage." In December 1975 the MPLA enacted another measure designed to bring the rebellious dockers under closer government control. It nationalized all docking enterprises in Luanda and stepped up its pressure on the dock workers to increase productivity.

Under the guise of installing a system of "workers' management," the MPLA also sought to tie the workers of various enterprises directly to the MPLA's bureaucratic apparatus and stifle any independent initiatives.

The MPLA sought to use the "people's power" bodies, neighborhood committees, and workers' commissions to extend its control over the entire population under the slogan of "discipline." Some of these groups had originally developed independently of the MPLA. Several neighborhood committees, for instance, arose after the July-August 1974 attacks on the muceques by armed settler gangs. The workers' commissions developed during the strike wave that began after the April 1974 Lisbon coup. But after the MPLA gained dominance in Luanda, these groups were either dissolved or transformed into bureaucratically controlled organs for imposing MPLA policies on the masses.

Le Monde correspondent René Lefort reported in the October 23 issue that the various self-defense organizations in Luanda's muceques had been disbanded, reorganized with "politically conscious elements" in the leadership, and then placed under the direct control of the MPLA military command. Any armed groups outside the MPLA's army or militia were declared illegal.

Lefort later reported, in the January 3, 1976, *Le Monde*, that several MPLA decrees specified that government officials were to follow the policies laid down by the MPLA's leading bodies. The function of the "people's power" groups, Lefort continued, was to execute decisions on a local level. To give them at least an appearance of having some authority, the groups were to be allowed to veto the *appointment* of local officials.

From the MPLA's own statements it appeared that the workers' commissions set up in some of the factories had been consigned to a similarly subordinate role. According to the MPLA's scheme, their chief function was to organize stepped-up production—not to represent the interests of the workers. In a speech published in the December 20, 1975, issue of *Vitória Certa*, an official organ of the MPLA, Neto declared that the MPLA faced a battle on two fronts. One was against the FNLA and UNITA and their backers; the other was "the battle of production, the battle of labor, for productivity, against laziness, against idleness, against sabotage of our rear lines."

Neto complained of "insufficient" work in the plants: "It seems that in some factories the workers' commissions have time and again failed in organizing production. . . ." He singled out the problems the MPLA continued to face at Luanda's port, denouncing the "so-called workers" who "sabotaged" the economy.

Neto also offered some advice to the workers: they should "not elect to the workers' commissions those who speak better, but those who work better. . . ."

In case the workers did not heed Neto's remarks, the same issue of *Vitória Certa* carried a series of articles describing what could happen to a workers' commission that did not follow MPLA policy. In Dondo, more than 100 miles southeast of Luanda, an MPLA Action Group at the SATEC factory, which employed 1,200 workers, had organized a campaign for the ouster of the existing workers' commissions. At an assembly held November 24, a motion was pushed through denouncing the "labor aristocracy" leadership of the commission for not solving the administrative problems of increasing production. The MPLA's subdelegate in Dondo said that "the worker comrades of SATEC are totally undisciplined, and the drop in production in this factory is caused by the indiscipline of the workers." He also told the SATEC workers that their allies included "the patriotic comrades of the national bourgeoisie."

The disciplining of the working class and the crushing of any independent organizations in Luanda was not limited to political pressure or manipulation. The MPLA also employed force. The January 2, 1976, issue of the French Trotskyist weekly *Rouge* reported that the neighborhood committee in the São Paulo area of Luanda was occupied in October by MPLA troops after they arrested nine of its members. Eleven other militants, *Rouge* reported, were arrested elsewhere. In November they were released and deported to Portugal. The Comites Amilcar Cabral, which were active in the "people's power" groups in Luanda, were crushed by the MPLA, and the newspaper *Poder Popular* was banned. This repression was carried out in the name of a campaign against "the partisans of Trotsky and Bakunin," *Rouge* reported.

Shortly after the proclamation of the People's Republic, the new MPLA justice minister, Diogenes Boavida, announced that "people's tribunals" would be set up first in Luanda and later throughout the country (assuming an MPLA victory). For those judged by "the will and decisions of the popular masses" and found guilty, labor camps were to be provided. The MPLA made it clear that the targets of this repression were not only members and supporters of the FNLA and UNITA. *Jeune Afrique* reported November 14:

> The MPLA has launched a major purge: It shut down the weekly *A Voz de Angola* and arrested a number of activists charged with leftism, as well as certain intellectuals who until recently were sympathizers of the Active Revolt and who have maintained a critical attitude toward the leadership of Agostinho Neto.
>
> Among the persons arrested was the journalist Joaquim de Castro Lopo, a former representative of the MPLA in Algiers and the editor of the daily *Jornal de Angola.* Since his arrest in late October, no one knows what has become of him. Warned by friends, the associate editor of the same newspaper, Ricardo Ferreira, and a twenty-one-year-old reporter managed to flee after reaching the airport hidden in an ambulance.

The MPLA Central Committee also enacted a law which could be used to deny Angolan citizenship to anyone collaborating with the FNLA and UNITA. To muzzle the press, it arrested or deported several foreign journalists in late 1975. Only dispatches based on official MPLA statements were allowed to be filed from Luanda during that period.

To better coordinate its repression, the MPLA established a new secret police body, the Angola Information and Security Directorate (DISA—Direcção de Informação e Segurança de Angola). The decree setting up the DISA declared that it was to combat "all actions and activities that are directed against the Constitution, the organs of the State and of the MPLA and its officials. . ." (*Jornal Novo*, January 2, 1976). In an interview in the December 26 *Le Monde*, Agostinho Neto declared that "measures will have to be taken to make sure that misguided elements can't interfere with our daily lives."

Although the People's Republic relied heavily on Soviet military equipment and several thousand Cuban troops in its war with the FNLA, UNITA, and their backers, the MPLA continued its efforts to solicit more support from the imperialist powers. This was an important feature of Neto's November 11 independence day speech; a dispatch in the November 12, 1975, *New York Times* reported that he "said foreign investment would be welcome from all abiding by Angolan laws." And the constitution enacted by the MPLA guaranteed the protection of private property, "including that of foreigners, so long as it benefits the economy of the country and is in the interests of the Angolan people."

The MPLA was successful, to some degree, in getting such imperialist aid. Arménio Ferreira, a member of the MPLA's coordinating bureau for Europe, explained in an interview shortly before independence day that "Sweden, Holland, Denmark, Norway, and even Belgium consider the MPLA as the only legitimate movement of the Angolan people. . . ." He later added, "Canada is another country that helps us a lot. . ." (*Diário de Notícias*, November 6, 1975).

Some of these countries began aiding the MPLA while it was still in the coalition with the FNLA and UNITA. After leading an MPLA delegation to Belgium and Holland in early 1975, Neto declared that the MPLA had secured material support from those two countries, "through their solidarity organisations, their political organisations and even their governments" (*Daily News*, Tanzania, April 9, 1975). In September 1975 the Danish government announced that it would extend 425,000 kroner (about US$70,000) in credits to the MPLA. That was only part of the aid package scheduled for the period up to November 11.

Washington's provision of millions of dollars in arms and other aid to the MPLA's rivals since the breakdown of the coalition in July 1975 did not appreciably affect the MPLA's approach toward the American economic interests operating in Angola. After a series of discussions with MPLA leaders, Mark Moran, an aide to Senator John V. Tunney, stated January 25, 1976: "But the people I spoke with went to great lengths to indicate that their position was not against the multinational companies, which they felt should operate here in a mutually profitable arrangement with the Government." In a dispatch from Luanda January 22, 1976, *New York Times* correspondent Michael T. Kaufman reported: "Dr. Neto and other leaders here have in their public statements developed an approach to the United States in which Secretary of State Henry Kissinger and his Angolan policies are depicted as advancing imperialist designs while the Senate and to some extent American companies that have holdings here are carefully praised."

Such praise for the American companies in Angola was not surprising, since one of them, Gulf Oil, had been a major source of income for the MPLA for several months (as it had previously been for the Portuguese during their war against the nationalists). Noting that "American elements are aiding and bankrolling opposing sides," David Anable reported in the December 15, 1975, *Christian Science Monitor*:

> Gulf Oil Company, which has oil wells in the MPLA-controlled enclave of Cabinda, has confirmed that it has handed over hundreds of millions of dollars this year in royalty and tax payments to the Luanda-based "tax collector of the State of Angola."
>
> The latest payment (about $100 million) was made in September when the MPLA was in full control of Luanda. MPLA finance minister Saydi Mingas, according to highly reliable sources, has confirmed receipt of this payment.

Gulf Oil's concerns in Angola were apparently different from those of the White House. Its main interest was in continuing to pump oil out of Cabinda. It also apparently feared that Washington's intervention in Angola could have driven the MPLA to take reprisals against U.S. economic interests. Gerald Bender commented in an article in the November 23, 1975, *Los Angeles Times*, "Gulf does not appear to share Kissinger's or [CIA Director] Colby's fear of the MPLA. Saydi Mingas, the MPLA finance minister in the transitional government, recently remarked in Washington that relations between his party and Gulf were 'very good.' The company does not perceive the MPLA to constitute a greater threat to its operations than the FNLA or UNITA. The oil company is concerned about U.S. intervention—a concern which has been quietly communicated to the State Department."

The State Department, in turn, was concerned that the Gulf payments to the MPLA could hamper Washington's efforts to bolster the MPLA's rivals. Under the department's pressure, Gulf announced December 22 that it had suspended its operations in Cabinda and would place further tax and royalty payments in a blocked account, to be paid to any regime in Angola that won formal international recognition.

Another imperialist economic interest that the MPLA apparently had "very good" relations with was Diamang, the South African, Belgian, British, Portuguese, and American owned consortium which exploits the vast diamond fields of northeastern Angola, an area controlled by the MPLA. Diamang had maintained a private security force of 500 troops which was dissolved after the April 1974 Lisbon coup. Citing João Martins, a Portuguese director of the company, Kaufman reported in the October 5, 1975, *New York Times*: "With the private army demobilized, Mr. Martins said, the company is relying on the protection of the Popular Movement for the Liberation of Angola. . . . Mr. Martins said he was most worried at the moment by recurring reports that troops of the National Front for the Liberation of Angola, headed by Holden Roberto, were massing on the border of Zaïre, which abuts the Diamang and supports Mr. Roberto."

Like Gulf, Martins also expressed optimism that Diamang would be able to continue operations under an MPLA regime: "Probably the cost of the concession will go up, but diamond mining is a highly technical enterprise, and our experience will be necessary to an independent Angola." Like Gulf, Diamang was also reported to have made tax and royalty payments to the MPLA, although the amount was not known.

The FNLA-UNITA Alliance

The regime set up by the FNLA and UNITA in Huambo (formerly Nova Lisboa), named the Democratic People's Republic of Angola, was a hasty response to the MPLA's establishment of a regime in Luanda. It was less of a government coalition than an uneasy military alliance of convenience against their common rival. In fact, judging by news reports from Huambo in the first months of the regime's existence, it appeared that the administration of the Democratic People's Republic was extremely disorganized or in many cases virtually nonexistent. This was partly the result of FNLA and UNITA's preoccupation with their military campaigns against the MPLA and of the fact that the MPLA had inherited almost the entire colonial administrative apparatus, centered in Luanda.

Whatever foreign exchange the country had at the time of independence was located in Luanda, the banking center. All communications with the outside world, moreover, had been routed through Luanda. In contrast, the Huambo regime was plagued by severe shortages of gasoline, food, and medical supplies, a breakdown of the city water supply, and the paralysis of the postal service and transportation system throughout the area. In addition, the light manufacturing plants, mines, and plantations in the central plateau area ceased to produce after the sudden departure of the Portuguese settlers.

A consolidation of the Huambo regime and a victory by the FNLA or UNITA would not have been any more in the interests of the Angolan masses than an MPLA victory. Both the FNLA and UNITA made repeated pledges to protect "private enterprise." They had shown during their participation in the Luanda coalition regime that they were just as willing as the MPLA to break strikes and destroy the independent neighborhood committees and workers' commissions.

The FNLA and UNITA also gave no indication that their methods of rule were any more proletarian or democratic than those of the MPLA. Their aim was likewise to control and discipline the Angolan masses. For instance, in August, UNITA Secretary-General Miguel Nzau Puna was quoted by *Jornal de Angola* as saying that all Angolans in UNITA-controlled territory were required to carry identity cards. These cards were to be checked by "control groups." A few days before the departure of the Portuguese, Jonas Savimbi called for the disarming of the Luanda population, indicating what might be in store for them if the UNITA were successful in "liberating" the city from the MPLA.

The FNLA also indicated its attitude toward the predominantly Mbundu supporters of the MPLA. After the FNLA suffered a series of setbacks in northern Angola in January 1976, Paulo Tuba, a member of the FNLA's Political Bureau, threatened terrorist actions against the MPLA and its backers, both within Angola and abroad. Speaking in Kinshasa January 14, he warned that the first such attacks would be "right in Luanda." In a reference to plastic explosives, he added: "We are prepared to plastic movies, markets and public places. . . . In a war of liberation people have to die."

In the interests of their own narrow factional struggle for power, the FNLA and UNITA actively collaborated with the American and South African intervention and thus endangered the entire Angolan struggle for independence. They allowed South African regular troops and American and European mercenaries recruited by the CIA to enter the country, thus assuming major responsibility for giving imperialism an opening for escalated intervention.

The FNLA and UNITA started receiving substantial amounts of Western military aid shortly after they were driven out of Luanda by the MPLA in mid-July. Speaking in Silva Porto, the capital of Bié district and the UNITA's military headquarters, Savimbi announced September 24 that his group had received important arms shipments from "certain Western democracies."

The arms and financial aid provided to the FNLA by Washington was funneled through the Mobutu regime in Zaïre.

While the FNLA and UNITA clearly collaborated with the imperialist intervention in Angola, they were not mere "puppets of international imperialism," as the MPLA characterized them. Both groups continued to maintain their bases among large sections of the Angolan population, the FNLA among the Bakongo in the north and the UNITA among the Ovimbundu in the central plateau area. Godwin Matatu reported in the November 1975 issue of *Africa* magazine that "Jonas Savimbi and his colleagues have been extensively touring their central and southern strongholds, attracting large crowds, to explain their case to the people." After the military column supported by white troops recaptured the port of Lobito from the MPLA in early November, Savimbi addressed a crowd reported to number tens of thousands of Ovimbundu in the central square of the city. Some of the rallies in UNITA territory have reportedly been as large as 100,000 persons.

In early July 1975, it was the FNLA minister of the interior, N'gola Kabangu, who was one of the first to warn of an imminent South African intervention in Angola. According to the July 8 *Jornal de Angola,* he said, "In Cunene we are aware of pretexts for invasion which South Africa searches for or fabricates. South Africa alleged that we have installed S.W.A.P.O. bases on our territory, that 5,000 Namibians are being trained in Angola and that these 5,000 men represent a danger to South Africa. Under such pretexts South Africa could invade Cunene some day. Attempts have been made, and shots have been exchanged between South African troops and members of UNITA. South African forces have penetrated deep into our territory in armored cars and withdrew only because the moment was not yet there."

When the South Africans did intervene in Angola in greater force about a month later, *Jornal de Angola,* by that time controlled by the MPLA, reported in its August 31 issue that South African troops had attacked *both* MPLA and UNITA positions on August 22.

After deciding for factional reasons to collaborate with the South Africans, the FNLA and UNITA came under increasing African diplomatic pressure. Idi Amin of Uganda, head of the Organization of African Unity, warned the two nationalist groups November 28 that African states "may have to review their positions on the Angolan situation and their attitude to your

two parties in particular" because of the South African intervention. (The OAU position at the time was to not recognize any of
the three groups and to press for negotiations among them.)

This pressure was undoubtedly the major factor behind
Savimbi's calls in late December 1975 and early January 1976 for
the withdrawal of South African forces from Angola. Pressure
from the ranks of the UNITA may also have been a factor. The
December 18 Lisbon daily *Jornal Novo* reported, "Jonas Savimbi
. . . in Kampala [Uganda] has just called on African states to
help him drive the South Africans out of his country. 'By asking
for this support,' he added, 'I have proven that I am not
collaborating with the racist regime of South Africa.'"

The UNITA's annual congress, which ended in Silva Porto
January 1, endorsed Savimbi's call for the ouster of the South
Africans. The congress also demanded the "immediate expul-
sion" from Angola of all forces of the Portuguese Liberation
Army (Exército de Libertação Portuguesa), a right-wing Portu-
guese terrorist group allied with Gen. António de Spínola. It
coupled these positions with a demand for the withdrawal of
Soviet and Cuban forces from the country.

Another sign of conflict between the UNITA and foreign troops
who were aiding it was the outbreak of fighting December 24
between forces of the UNITA and the "Chipenda Brigade." The
brigade was led by Daniel Chipenda, the former MPLA leader
who joined the FNLA in early 1975. According to the December
27 *Jornal Novo,* it was composed almost entirely of white troops,
many of them mercenaries, from Angola, Mozambique, and
Portugal.

According to later reports, Chipenda's forces were engaged in
widespread looting. The fighting reportedly began when troops of
the UNITA attacked Chipenda's headquarters and other installations of the brigade in Huambo in order to discipline them.
Calling Chipenda a "reactionary" and blaming him for the
fighting, Savimbi said that twenty UNITA troops had died in the
battles. Other battles between UNITA and Chipenda followed.

In conjunction with its diplomatic campaign before the opening
of an OAU summit meeting in January, the UNITA also made a
series of overtures to the MPLA. Several UNITA leaders declared
that they were willing to open negotiations, without setting any
prior conditions. The UNITA congress characterized the MPLA
as "a brother who has been led from his true path, and not a
mortal enemy." Paulo Tchipilica, the UNITA's representative in

Lisbon, said that the UNITA and MPLA were "both progressive and patriotic movements." While conceding that the FNLA "could not be ignored" in any new coalition regime, he added, "Ideologically, we are much closer to the MPLA."

Like the MPLA, the FNLA also continued to receive military aid from bureaucratized workers' states. After Angola gained its independence Peking had withdrawn its military mission from Zaïre, where Chinese instructors had trained FLNA troops, but their function had been taken over by a North Korean training mission.

Meanwhile, as the internecine warfare grew, U.S. imperialism had begun to find renewed opportunities for intervention in Angola.

The CIA's "Operation Angola"

On January 3, 1976, President Gerald Ford announced that he was only interested in giving the Angolans "an opportunity to make the decision for themselves" on who should run their country. And in case anyone questioned the White House's proclaimed lack of self-interest, Ford could have pointed to the massive CIA operation he had authorized several months earlier in order to help the Angolans make their "own" choice. Not to mention Washington's previous aid to the Salazarist dictatorship, in which similar considerations were no doubt involved.

After having "reactivated" the flow of CIA funds, about $300,000, to Holden Roberto in January 1975, and after having sent a similar amount to the UNITA several months later, the White House carried out a major review of the Angolan situation in July, at the time of the breakdown of the coalition regime in Luanda. The review was conducted by the high-level intelligence coordinating body called the "Forty Committee," the subcommittee of the National Security Council that has the responsibility of approving all proposals for covert intelligence activities carried out abroad. In addition to Kissinger, who chaired it, the committee was composed of CIA Director William Colby, Deputy Secretary of Defense William Clement, and Chairman of the Joint Chiefs of Staff Gen. George S. Brown. The Forty Committee decided to send $10 million worth of supplies to Angola.

By December, this figure had risen to $25 million, with an additional $7 million "in the pipeline." But these figures were just the official ones. The House Select Committee in Intelligence, which at the time was conducting investigations into the CIA's operations, announced January 19 that the CIA systematically undervalued the military equipment it sent to Angola. A .45-caliber automatic pistol, for instance, was listed for as little as $5, and a .30-caliber carbine at $7.55.

Some of the aid was directly allotted to the FNLA and UNITA. But in the initial months of the CIA operations, when Washington did not want American arms to be seen in Angola, the White House also gave funds to President Mobutu Sese Seko of Zaïre to buy arms for the FNLA and UNITA from various European countries, particularly Belgium. In addition, the White House proposed sending $60 million in financial and military aid to the Mobutu regime for fiscal 1976; of that amount, $20 million was for "Security Supporting Assistance," a category designed to "support or promote economic or political stability." When Kissinger was asked, during hearings on U.S. aid to Zaïre before the Senate Appropriations Committee November 20, whether Washington was helping Mobutu "do whatever he was doing in Angola," Kissinger replied: yes.

Much of the American armament destined directly for the MPLA's rivals was also funneled through Zaïre. According to a "high-ranking Government official" cited by David Binder in the December 12 *New York Times,* the American supplies were flown aboard U.S. C-141 Starlifter transport planes to landing fields in Zaïre, where they were turned over to the Zaïrean army. "American military supplies have consisted mainly of portable infantry weapons, the official said, including large numbers of antitank missile launchers and antipersonnel rocket launchers—'the kind you hold on your shoulder that you could use with a minimum of training.' " The official also claimed that there were "no American advisers in Angola, either civilian or military." He admitted, however, that Washington had supplied five artillery spotter planes that flew over Angolan battle zones and returned to bases in Zaïre; their American pilots "fly in and out," he said.

The CIA did not limit itself to providing arms and money. In a move reminiscent of its covert operations in Laos in the 1960s, the CIA began the recruitment of an undercover army composed of American and European mercenaries to fight in Angola against the MPLA. The first major revelation of the CIA's role was a front-page article in the January 2 *Christian Science Monitor.* Staff writer David Anable reported that, according to "senior mercenary officers" who were "close" to the agency "the CIA is indirectly recruiting American ex-servicemen, training them, dispatching them to southern Africa, contributing toward their pay . . . and providing them and the indigenous forces with light and heavy weaponry." The mercenaries were apparently recruited through fake private companies operating as fronts, a technique commonly used by the CIA.

Significantly, South African newspapers disclosed the American mercenary operation several weeks before the *Christian Science Monitor* did. For instance, the December 6, 1975, issue of the South African *Star Weekly* reported from New York City: "Scores of American mercenaries are fighting in Angola and hundreds more are expected to be signed up in the United States in the next few days." One of the recruiters, David Bufkin, a former U.S. paratrooper, worked through connections in New York City, Johannesburg, and Salisbury, Rhodesia. Bufkin said that he and fellow recruiters in Los Angeles, Chicago, New York, and other U.S. cities were offering $1,200 a month.

The *Star Weekly* quoted another recruiter as saying, "We don't know who is bankrolling this thing. . . . There are a lot of potential sources—South African, Zaire and Portuguese businessmen . . . and somewhere along the line there may even be some American money."

As early as mid-November, *Intercontinental Press* correspondent Tony Hodges reported seeing an American mercenary in Angola and was told that another fifteen Americans were serving as instructors for the UNITA at its training camp near Silva Pôrto.

Anable reported that at the time there were already 300 American mercenaries operating in Angola. Most of them were with the UNITA forces in the southern and central areas, although one unit was working with the FNLA in the north. A second group of about 300 American mercenaries, almost all Vietnam veterans, had also reportedly been recruited in the United States. Anable said that according to his sources, half of them had undergone a refresher training course at Fort Benning, Georgia. The second group was waiting for additional CIA funds before embarking for Angola at the time Anable filed his report.

Some of the Americans were directly recruited from among active U.S. servicemen. Citing "high State Department sources," Sean Gervasi, an adviser to the Center for National Security Studies, revealed at a December 19, 1975, press conference that "numbers of U.S. mercenaries have been allowed to reach Angola and to enter combat. It is reported that some of these mercenaries have come from regular units by volunteering and that they leave behind them letters of resignation from the regular forces in case such letters should be needed. Regular commissioned and noncommissioned officers have been approaching enlisted men to ask whether they might be interested in volunteering."

In addition to the mercenary operation, at least eight CIA agents were reported to be in Angola. According to the CBS television network in its December 17 evening news program, the CIA was supervising the distribution of military supplies in Silva Pôrto and Uige (formerly Carmona). Citing "an eyewitness to operations in Angola," Senator John Tunney stated January 6, 1976, that American pilots had also been airlifting weapons into Angola from Zaïre. "They have been flying four to five missions a day in American-built C-130 Hercules cargo carriers," he said. Employees of a American aircraft company, Tunney added, had "already come under fire while flying in a helicopter near Luanda in Angola."

When asked about such reports, White House Press Secretary Ron Nessen replied January 2 that no U.S. government agency was recruiting or training American mercenaries for Angola. He also claimed that he did not know if mercenary recruiting was being carried out by any "private company." When asked if Fort Benning was being used to train mercenaries or if Cuban exiles in the United States were being recruited, Nessen refused to answer. Ford followed this performance with one of his own the next day. "The United States is not training foreign mercenaries in Angola," he claimed. "We do expend some federal funds—or United States funds—in trying to be helpful, but we are not training foreign mercenaries." He would not deny, however, that the government was providing funds for that purpose.

During congressional hearings on covert CIA operations and on the U.S. involvement in Angola, both then CIA Director Colby and Ford's nominee to replace him, George Bush, stressed that covert CIA "paramilitary" operations could not be ruled out.

Reviving the Domino Theory

In an effort to gain public support for U.S. aggression in Angola, White House officials tried to whip up cold war fears of "Communist expansionism." But by echoing the justifications presented in the opening days of American military intervention against the Vietnamese people, they only succeeded in creating a ripple of fear of a new Vietnam War.

Referring to the Soviet support given to the MPLA, Kissinger declared at a November 10, 1975, news conference that Washington would not tolerate Soviet "hegemonial aspirations" in Angola. He termed the Angolan war a "grave problem" and warned that Moscow's policy "was not compatible with the spirit of détente." Kissinger's warnings soon became more pointed; he said November 24 that "the United States cannot remain indifferent" to Soviet and Cuban military involvement. "We cannot ignore, for example, the substantial Soviet buildup of weapons in Angola, which has introduced great-power rivalry into Africa for the first time in fifteen years." Kissinger urged Moscow to exercise "restraint," and warned of the consequences of not doing so: "Time is running out; continuation of an interventionist policy must inevitably threaten other relationships." Washington, he said, would "never permit détente to turn into a subterfuge of unilateral advantage."

Daniel P. Moynihan, the U.S. ambassador to the United Nations, was particularly eloquent on the question of Soviet "hegemonial aspirations." If Washington were unable to "proceed properly" in Angola, he said, "the Communists would take over Angola and will thereby considerably control the oil shipping lanes from the Persian Gulf to Europe. They will be next to Brazil. They will have a large chunk of Africa, and the world will be different in the aftermath if they succeed" (quoted in the *Washington Post,* December 18, 1975).

In arguing his case before Congress for continued U.S. aid for the FNLA and UNITA, Kissinger presented a variant of the old "domino theory." He pointed to the dominoes bordering on Angola—Washington's allies in Zaïre, Zambia, and South Africa. And if Washington did not stop Moscow in Angola, he said, the Kremlin could be encouraged to press its political interests in other parts of the world. As if to provide an example of this, Kissinger, according to the January 9 *New York Times,* "reportedly told. . .visiting Israeli officials that if the United States, because of Congressional opposition, failed to halt Soviet military activities in Angola, the Soviet Union and others might not take American warnings seriously in the future. In Mr. Kissinger's view, this could encourage Arab countries such as Syria to run risks that could lead to a new attack on Israel, backed up by the Russians."

In a warning to the Senate not to cut off U.S. funds for the CIA Angola operation, the *Wall Street Journal,* in a December 19,

1975, editorial, also focused on this aspect of the potential consequences for Washington if it did not halt "the neo-colonialist
Soviet thrust in Africa":

> Yet when all the economic, military and strategic considerations are
> set aside, the Soviet challenge in Angola is primarily directed at the
> U.S. and is primarily psychological. Clearly the Soviets are in Angola
> and elsewhere testing American resolve in the light of the post-Vietnam
> reassessment here and the movement of the world military balance in
> the Soviets' favor. The American reaction will no doubt influence the
> extent of further testing.
>
> That is by no means an argument for an open-ended commitment in
> Angola or elsewhere. The costs and benefits need to be balanced, but
> $60 million in arms isn't much of a cost. If the United States publicly
> declares itself unwilling to take even small risks to limit Soviet
> expansionism, it will be an open invitation to even bolder challenges
> throughout the world.

What such statements reflected was not so much a fear of
Soviet military advances, but concern that by gaining increased
political influence in Angola and the rest of Africa, Moscow could
strengthen its bargaining hand within the framework of the
détente. This consideration was evident during hearings before
the Senate Foreign Relations Subcommittee on Africa November
6; Colby and Undersecretary of State Joseph J. Sisco tried to
justify the U.S. aid to the MPLA's rivals, as well as to the regimes
in Zaïre, Ethiopia, and Kenya, on the grounds that Washington
needed "bargaining chips" with the Soviet Union.

In the first major revelation of American intervention in
Angola, Leslie H. Gelb reported in the September 25, 1975, *New
York Times* that "four official sources" told him "the main
purpose for the covert American effort in Angola was to underline
the Administration's support for President Mobutu, the man on
whom Secretary of State Henry Kissinger is banking to oppose
Moscow's interests in Africa and to further Washington's
interests in various international forums." The Mobutu regime in
Zaïre also had its own interests to advance in Angola. Despite
official denials, Mobutu appeared to covet the oil fields of
Cabinda, as well as its port, which could have given Zaïre
improved access to the ocean. Zaïre also transported about 35
percent of its copper, its principal export, through Angola along
the Benguela railway. And having backed the FNLA for years,

Mobutu may have feared that a victorious MPLA might provide sanctuary for rebels hostile to his regime.

For its part, Moscow's massive arms shipments to the MPLA were not designed to weaken capitalism in Angola or to aid the struggle against continued imperialist domination—a fact that Washington was well aware of. The aim was to strengthen the wing of the Angolan nationalist movement that the Kremlin considered the most favorable to its foreign policy objectives. Even such bourgeois dictators as Idi Amin of Uganda and Indira Gandhi of India receive massive military and economic aid from Moscow in its efforts to buy political favor.

For the American and European imperialists, Angola's vast deposits of oil and minerals represented a particularly valuable prize. If the Kremlin gained strong political influence over the new Angolan regime—a possibility if the MPLA won through heavy Soviet and Cuban backing—its diplomatic hand would be greatly strengthened. And by appearing to oppose the American and South African intervention, the Kremlin could increase its stature among nationalist currents throughout Africa and the rest of the world. The Soviet Stalinists would then have better leverage in bargaining with Washington and Western Europe for more favorable terms within the détente.

Moscow's opportunist motives in backing the MPLA become particularly evident when the quantity of its recent military aid is compared with that allotted in the past. It was estimated that about $110 million worth of Soviet arms had been given to the MPLA during 1975, that is, since the struggle between the nationalist groups reached the stage of major armed conflict. During the entire fourteen-year period when the MPLA was battling Portuguese colonialism, Moscow provided only $54 million.

Although Washington also publicly blasted the Cuban involvement in Angola, the State Department did not appear too concerned; it was viewed as subsidiary to Moscow's role. A major Cuban function was reportedly to operate the sophisticated equipment Moscow sent the MPLA and train Angolans to use it, thereby relieving the Kremlin of the diplomatic hazards of sending in Soviet military advisers. Havana, through its involvement against the South Africans and Americans, also stood to gain through reinforcement of its anti-imperialist image.

Although Washington wanted to prevent the Kremlin from picking up a valuable "bargaining chip" in Angola, it was not prepared to scuttle the détente to do so. Kissinger's trip to Moscow in January to continue the Strategic Arms Limitation Talks with the Soviet leaders was an indication that both Washington and Moscow were trying to prevent their Angola dispute from upsetting détente.

In their justifications for the U.S. intervention, CIA and State Department officials made it clear that they did not consider the MPLA a threat to imperialist holdings. For instance, at his December 23 news conference Kissinger said: "We are not opposed to the M.P.L.A. as such. . . . We can live with any of the factions in Angola. . . ." CIA officials voiced the view that "the differences in government should the MPLA win would be minimal" (cited by Senator Tunney, *Congressional Record,* December 17, 1975, p. S22539).

Washington, however, was not interested in seeing any of the Angolan nationalist groups "win" the civil war. By funneling arms and money to the FNLA and UNITA, it sought not merely to prevent any MPLA victory, but also to perpetuate the war—with the aim of wearing down all three groups, weakening the entire independence movement, and forcing the nationalists to make further concessions to imperialism.

The White House Faces a Roadblock

The fear that the CIA's intervention in Angola might escalate into a new Vietnam War—despite administration assurances that its aims were "limited"—produced a rapid reaction not only among the U.S. public but within the government itself. In fact, differences over how far to go in Angola emerged inside the Ford administration several months before the extent of the intervention became public.

Bender pointed out in his November 23 *Los Angeles Times* article that "Kissinger has little support for his policy within his own African bureau. After a thorough review of the Angolan situation within the State Department this past June, the bureau almost unanimously recommended that the United States stay out of the conflict."

The divisions became so sharp that Nathaniel Davis resigned in August as assistant secretary of state for African affairs. Davis reportedly favored seeking a diplomatic "settlement" in Angola and playing no "active" role in the civil war. Seymour M. Hersh reported in the December 14 *New York Times* that Davis had sent a "steady stream of memoranda" to Kissinger. "An official" cited by Hersh explained: "First of all, Davis told them that it won't work. Neither Savimbi or Roberto are good fighters—in fact, they couldn't fight their way out of a paper bag. It's the wrong game and the players we got are losers." Davis also argued, according to the official, that when the U.S. intervention in Angola failed, such American supporters in Africa as Mobutu of Zaïre and Kaunda of Zambia would be injured, leaving Washington with South Africa as its only ally in the region.

Similar considerations lay behind a December 19 Senate vote on a defense appropriations bill barring use of funds "for any activities in Angola other than intelligence gathering." The vote was 54 to 22, and marked a significant opposition by both Democrats and Republicans to Kissinger and Ford's war plans. The House of Representatives, on January 27, also voted to block such funds.

Before the Senate vote, some senators questioned just how much influence Moscow would gain in Angola if the MPLA did win. Richard Clark, chairman of the Foreign Relations Subcommittee on Africa, who had met with leaders of the MPLA several months earlier, said he had been convinced that if the MPLA won, it would "within a year be pursuing a nonaligned policy independent of the Russians."

The MPLA sought to encourage such a view in Washington, frequently stating that its foreign policy would be "nonaligned." Article 6 of the constitution enacted by the MPLA regime stated that "the People's Republic of Angola will not join any international military organization, nor allow the installation of foreign military bases on its national territory." Even if Moscow did make a significant diplomatic gain through an MPLA victory, the Angolan regime could quickly shift toward Western sources of aid as long as it remained based on capitalist property relations. The Kremlin's allocation of billions of dollars in military and financial aid to the Egyptian government did not prevent President Anwar el-Sadat from seeking a better deal with Washington.

This debate within U.S. ruling circles represented only tactical differences over what course would best serve the interests of American imperialism. But the outbreak of the debate at the very beginning of the enewed American involvement in Angola was significant. Such differences over Vietnam did not arise until after Washington had unsuccessfully committed hundreds of thousands of troops and a massive antiwar movement had developed within the United States. With the memory of Vietnam and recent CIA scandals still fresh, the American population was sensitive to military adventures abroad. A sector of the ruling class recognized this, and feared that a major intervention in Angola would be met by massive opposition from the start. Such an antiwar movement could have grown even broader than the one against the Vietnam War, with far greater active participation by Black people. So they asked themselves, Are the risks of intervening in Angola worth it?

The European Connection

The administration's response to public and Congressional opposition was to press ahead, while also shifting in some cases to less direct and visible forms of intervention.

The administration's determination was pointedly reaffirmed by Kissinger December 23, just four days after the Senate barred additional funds for the CIA's Angolan operations. He proclaimed that the White House was "going to make a major effort [in Angola], both diplomatically and on the ground. . . ." Complaining that the Senate vote "severely complicated" White House plans, Kissinger said the administration would use $9 million it had left to continue backing the MPLA's rivals.

At the time of the Senate vote, the White House indicated that only about $4 million remained in the CIA's "contingency fund" for covert operations. An unnamed U.S. official, however, told a reporter for the *New York Times* December 28 that more money had been "found." In early January, CIA Director Colby called it "the height of absurdity to say that CIA should not give some help" to the anti-MPLA groups.

The "diplomatic" effort Kissinger spoke of was the dispatching of his new assistant secretary of state for African affairs, William E. Schaufele, on a tour of several African and European countries in an attempt to block formal recognition of the MPLA regime by the Organization of African Unity, which opened an emergency summit meeting on Angola January 10 in Addis Ababa, Ethiopia. President Ford sent letters to a number of African heads of state, including Brig. Murtala Muhammed of Nigeria, "suggesting" that they not call on the OAU to recognize the MPLA. The White House enlisted the aid of several of its

European allies in this effort. West German Foreign Minister Hans-Dietrich Genscher sent letters to twelve African heads of state, and British Foreign Minister James Callaghan was reported to have done likewise. Paris sought to influence the position of some of its former African colonies. This diplomatic mobilization was prompted by Washington's fear that OAU recognition of the MPLA's People's Republic of Angola as the sole "legitimate" regime would hamper its efforts to get other members of NATO, some of which have important economic and political interests in Black African countries, to take on a greater role in funneling arms and money to the FNLA and UNITA.

Ford's arrogant pressure tactics received a hostile public reply in Nigeria. External Affairs Commissioner Col. Joseph Garba pledged to keep pressing for the MPLA's recognition; government-owned newspapers carried such headlines as "To Hell With America" and "Shut Up"; and about 2,000 protesters demonstrated outside the U.S. embassy in Lagos January 11. But Ford and Kissinger were successful in gaining a diplomatic victory when the OAU failed to formally condemn the South African and American intervention. The OAU also did not recognize the MPLA regime as Washington had feared.

Administration officials in Washington tried to use the OAU impasse as a justification for continued American activity in Angola, claiming that nearly half the OAU member states "supported" Washington's role. Schaufele, for instance, declared January 13 that "twenty-two African countries do support our policy." Within hours of the OAU summit's adjournment, White House Press Secretary Ron Nessen said that Ford would continue to provide "a limited amount of assistance" to those African regimes that were opposed to the MPLA.

Following the exposure of the CIA's mercenary operation by *Christian Science Monitor* reporter David Anable on January 2, the recruitment was shifted to Europe. Citing "sources close to the U.S. Central Intelligence Agency," Anable reported in the January 5 issue that European mercenaries were being hired through unnamed African embassies in several European capitals and were being paid with funds from the United States and other countries.

After the Senate vote blocking the Angola funds, Kissinger pledged "to generate as much support from other countries as we can." Some of Washington's NATO allies quickly rallied to its aid. Jim Hoagland reported in the December 24 *Washington Post* that the French secret police agency, SDECE (Service de Documentation Extérieure et de Contre-Espionage—Foreign Intelligence and Counterespionage Service), was channeling money and arms to the FNLA. This operation, Hoagland said, was carried out in cooperation with the CIA and with the approval of President Valéry Giscard d'Estaing. "SDECE's interests in Angola seem to be largely strategic," Hoagland said, "although there is a healthy dose of economic self-interest involved. The French share American concern about the spread of Communism and Soviet influence in Africa, and are interested in building their influence in Zaire and maintaining it in South Africa. . . ."

Moreover, Jacques Foccart, a key French intelligence figure in Africa for years, was reportedly supplying arms and money—and had promised mercenaries—to the Cabindan separatist group FLEC (Frente de Libertação do Enclave de Cabinda—Cabinda Liberation Front). Several FLEC leaders were thought to have close contacts with the French oil company Essences et Lubrifiants de France, which has a subsidiary in the Congo Republic (Brazzaville) near Cabinda. (Foccart was no stranger to such operations in Africa; he supplied French mercenaries to the Biafran secessionist regime during the Nigerian civil war.)

Washington's British allies were not to be left behind. John Marks revealed in an article reprinted in the December 16, 1975, *Congressional Record* that London had supplied the UNITA forces with British-made communications equipment. According to a report in the December 10 *Washington Post,* two British pilots working for the UNITA said arms were flown to the airport at Silva Pôrto aboard planes of Pearl Air, a chartered airline headquartered in the British colony of Hong Kong.

The January 11 *Sunday Telegraph* of London reported that according to "diplomatic sources" in southern Africa, dozens of British mercenaries were in Angola. "The Britons and other European mercenaries," reporter Norman Kirkham said, "have entered Angola secretly over the last few months. Recruitment is being stepped up to check military gains by the Russian-backed forces of the Popular Movement, M.P.L.A." The White House's most important ally in the imperialist intervention in Angola, however, was not a European government. It was the South African regime.

South Africa:
NATO's Secret Partner

Although the White House publicly denied any direct contact between U.S. officials and the racist regime in Pretoria concerning South Africa's intervention, the collaboration between the two imperialist powers in Angola was so apparent that UN Ambassador Daniel Moynihan felt he had to try to minimize it. He stated December 14, 1975, that there was only a "convergence in policy" between the two governments; while still denying any coordination of the U.S. and South African operations, he added, "We are doing the same thing, sort of."

But the fact that Washington and Pretoria were fighting on the same side in Angola was no mere coincidence or temporary "convergence." In fact, behind the absence of open, formal military relations between the two powers, and behind the smokescreen of periodic denunciations of apartheid by U.S. officials at the UN, lies an intricate and increasingly coordinated network of military contacts and alliances between Pretoria and its U.S. and European allies.

While trying to keep the fact as secret as possible, Washington has backed the white regime in Pretoria and its racist system of apartheid for years, just as it supported the Lisbon regime throughout the 1960s and early 1970s to protect U.S. capitalist interests in the area. Until the April 1974 Lisbon coup, in fact, the two policies were closely interrelated.

This U.S. commitment to Pretoria escalated sharply in the late 1960s. According to an article by Sean Gervasi, "The Politics of 'Accelerated Economic Growth'" (in *Change in Contemporary South Africa*), "Britain, the United States and other powers are not opposed to change in southern Africa, but they are opposed to change which they cannot control. In 1968 and 1969 they became exceedingly worried about the prospect of an upheaval in the region that they considered to have 'deteriorated' quite suddenly. They could not, as they saw it, stand idly by while the liberation movements dismantled, piece by piece, the whole structure of White power in the industrial heartland of Africa."

Washington and London, as leaders of the Western powers, decided on a three-pronged strategy for southern Africa, according to Gervasi. The first was to try to encourage some "reforms" in order to defuse the discontent in the area before it became too explosive. "Second," Gervasi continued, "they resolved to strengthen the White powers so that they would be better able to meet the military challenge posed by the liberation movements. This obviously had to be done very discreetly. Finally, they began to prepare the way for more direct and substantial military assistance to the White regimes. This was essentially contingency planning. It nonetheless reflected a definite commitment to go to the assistance of the White regimes in the event of a major crisis."

Although Washington and the West European powers have important interests to protect in Angola, their interests in South Africa are much more strategic. The racist regime is a bastion of imperialist power in Africa. South Africa controls the vital sea route around the Cape of Good Hope, past which much of the world's trade is shipped, including an estimated 7 million tons of Middle Eastern oil en route to Europe each day (about half the oil consumption of the European NATO powers). The Cape route retains its importance even after the reopening of the Suez Canal, which is too shallow to allow passage of the giant oil tankers.

South Africa also has some of the largest naval bases bordering on the Indian Ocean. Noting that "South African port facilities are of long-term strategic importance" and "the best in Africa," Kissinger's policy study of southern Africa concluded that "their availability to the Navy would be useful in peacetime and essential in time of war."

An August 1971 report submitted to the State Department by the African Affairs Advisory Council pointed out another reason for the area's strategic value to the imperialists. As quoted in the introduction to the Spokesman Books edition of the Kissinger study, it said: "Africa contains a major proportion of the world's reserves of a few commodities important to US strategic or economic needs. In the future, the US will probably have to look to Africa for, among other products, its chromite, platinum group metals, tantalite, petalite, gold, long-fibered amosite and crocido-lite asbestos, natural industrial diamond stones and phosphate rock (in 20-30 years) . . . most of these key minerals are found in southern Africa." South Africa also has important deposits of nickel and manganese, and, if the occupied territory of Namibia is included, controls 26 percent of the world's uranium reserves.

The American share in the exploitation of these resources has grown rapidly over the past few years. The October 1975 issue of *South African Scope,* a monthly published by the South African consulate in New York, pointed out:

> Three hundred and sixty U.S. enterprises have a direct investment of over $1.2-billion in South Africa—an increase of 100% over the past ten years.
>
> The U.S. is South Africa's second largest trading partner and American investments in South Africa continue to increase by 12.8 per cent a year.
>
> Just how important South Africa is regarded by the Americans as a market for investment is seen in the fact that South Africa is one of fewer than a score of countries with more than $1,000-million in direct American investment.
>
> What is more, Department of Commerce figures show that the American stake in the South African economy is growing at a rate that will double the investment in under ten years. . . .

The value of South African exports to the United States in 1974 stood at $650 million, a 74 percent increase over 1973 and more than twice the figure in 1972. South Africa's imports from the United States rocketed to $1200 million in 1974, up 55.4 percent from the previous year and nearly twice the amount imported in 1972. One of the major attractions for American investors in South Africa is the extremely low wages paid to Black workers, who are denied any union rights and whose wages are kept depressed by the rigid apartheid restrictions on Black labor. In 1967, for instance, the average rate of profit on all U.S. corporate investments in South Africa was about 19.2 percent, about double that on investments in other parts of the world (which in turn are more profitable than those within the United States).

South Africa's economic value is also a major consideration for Washington's imperialist competitors in Europe. Britain, with 60 percent of all foreign investments as of 1974, remains the largest investor in South Africa. In addition to the United States, however, Britain's position is being challenged by French, West German, and Japanese capital.

"Tar Baby" and After

The "tilt" toward the white minority regimes of southern Africa adopted by Nixon in February 1970 was designed to help Washington protect these strategic and economic interests.

Kissinger's study of southern Africa proposed several possible options; the one adopted, which became known as Tar Baby, included the following suggested moves:

—Enforce arms embargo against South Africa but with liberal treatment of equipment which could serve either military or civilian purposes.

—Permit US naval calls in South Africa with arrangements for non-discrimination toward US personnel in organised activity ashore; authorise routine use of airfields.

—Retain tracking stations in South Africa as long as required.

—Remove constraints on EXIM Bank facilities for South Africa; actively encourage US exports and facilitate US investment consistent with the Foreign Direct Investment Program.

—Conduct selected exchange programs with South Africa in all categories, including military.

—Without changing the US legal position that South African occupancy of South West Africa is illegal, we would play down the issue and encourage accommodation between South Africa and the UN. (British spellings retained from Spokesman edition, pp. 67-68.)

The only one of these suggestions that the White House did not follow in subsequent years was the second, on U.S. naval calls at South African ports. Such a move would have been extremely visible and could have led to protests by Blacks in the United States—or on board the U.S. ships themselves.

In early 1970, when the White House adopted the Tar Baby policy, the National Security Council also decided, in coordination with NATO, to bolster its military positions along the shores of the Indian Ocean against a possible increase in Soviet naval activity. That decision, combined with the steps taken by individual NATO members to protect their military and economic interests in southern Africa, led to a more synchronized "tilt" by NATO as a whole toward the South African regime.

A resolution passed by a meeting of the NATO Assembly in Bonn, West Germany, in November 1972 recommended to the NATO Ministerial Council that it give SACLANT (Supreme Allied Commander, Atlantic) "authority to plan for the protection of NATO Europe's vital shipping lines in the Indian Ocean and the South Atlantic including surveillance and communications." In May 1974 a NATO press secretary admitted that SACLANT had been given authorization to conduct such contingency planning. The instructions to SACLANT, which is based in Norfolk, Virginia, were issued by the NATO Defense Planning Committee in June 1973.

Michael J. Berlin reported in the May 10, 1974, *New York Post,* that "SACLANT has reached the conclusion that NATO itself does not have sufficient forces to deal with that area. And the corollary to this is that a defense arrangement involving the white minority regimes of southern Africa, South Africa in particular, is required."

An unnamed NATO official, quoted in a report prepared by Sean Gervasi, L.W. Bowman, and Ellen Frey-Wouters for the UN's decolonization committee in early 1974, said that the contingency planning was designed to make it possible "to go to the aid of our potential allies in southern Africa if the need should arise." The NATO press secretary who revealed the SACLANT authorization said that the planners were considering options not only for wartime but for "crisis situations" as well.

NATO's moves toward broadening its area of operations to include southern Africa were formalized at the June 1974 annual meeting of the Ministerial Council in Ottawa. Although the NATO region was defined in 1940 as including Europe, North America, the North Sea, and the North Atlantic (above the Tropic of Cancer), the Ottawa Declaration pointed out that NATO "interests can be affected by events in other areas of the world." In an article in the October 1974 *Esquire,* former *New York Times* reporter Tad Szulc commented: "This, of course, is a carte blanche for N.A.T.O. to become involved wherever it wishes. It may mean the Middle East, or the Indian Ocean—or southern Africa. The uncertainty is whether the United States and some of its allies, encouraged by the license issued in Ottawa, may choose to regard South Africa's internal security in the face of black pressures as a justification for direct air or naval support, using SACLANT's contingency planning."

The Portuguese coup of April 1974 unexpectedly led to the end of direct white rule in Angola and Mozambique, prompting the imperialists to press forward with their plans to bolster the remaining white regimes. "My own impression from Washington conversations," Szulc said, "is that SACLANT and the Pentagon planners will proceed with their contingency planning, perhaps with even greater urgency than before."

The ties between NATO and South Africa, however, did not remain merely in the planning stages. Pretoria, with the help of various NATO governments, actively began preparing to assume a greater military role in line with the NATO plans.

On September 1, 1974, it was revealed that the NATO Military Committee had decided to negotiate with Pretoria for the possible use of the giant Simonstown naval base near Cape Town for NATO warships (*Anti-Apartheid News,* May 1975). Pretoria subsequently launched a program to expand its port facilities far beyond the needs of the South African navy.

Closely related was Project Advocaat, a highly sophisticated and far-ranging communications and surveillance center located at Silvermine in the mountains north of Simonstown. The installation can cover a radius of about 5,000 miles, including much of the Indian Ocean, almost all of the South Atlantic, and the entire African continent. The system, according to a naval officer at the center cited in the July 31, 1975, *Wall Street Journal,* is linked via the Indian Ocean island of Mauritius to Hong Kong, Singapore, New Zealand, and Australia, and by way of the British Admiralty in London to the U.S. naval communications station in Derry, Northern Ireland, and from there to the United States. Also by way of the British Admiralty, the system is tied into NATO headquarters in Brussels.

The UN Special Committee on Apartheid acquired a set of documents from the British Anti-Apartheid Movement detailing part of NATO's direct involvement in Project Advocaat. *Africa* magazine reported in its July 1975 issue that, according to the documents, South African officials used NATO computers to calculate the types and quantities of spare parts that would be needed for Silvermine. They also utilized NATO's purchasing apparatus to buy equipment from such countries as Denmark and the Netherlands, which had publicly refused to sell arms to

Pretoria in the past. French, British, and American parts were also ordered for the project. The West German Defense Ministry helped Pretoria re-route some of the supplies from "unfriendly" NATO countries.

High-level contacts between South African military and government officials and their counterparts in Europe and the United States also multiplied. In January 1974, Cornelius P. Mulder, South African minister of information and of the interior (who was considered a possible successor to Prime Minister Vorster), spent five days in Washington. He met with then Vice-President Ford, various Congressional leaders, and Vice Adm. Ray Peet, a top Pentagon planner with responsibility for the Indian Ocean. Mulder made another trip to the United States in June 1975.

A month after the April 1974 Portuguese coup, Adm. Hugo H. Biermann, commander in chief of the South African military, also visited Washington—after Kissinger overruled a recommendation of the African Bureau of the State Department that he be denied a visa. Biermann met with J. William Middendorf, acting secretary of the navy, and Adm. Thomas H. Moorer, chairman of the Joint Chiefs of Staff. According to Szulc, Biermann dined with seventeen American admirals at the home of a Maryland Republican congressman. In March 1975 three members of Congress, two of whom happened to be on the House Armed Services Committee, visited South Africa. Among the figures they met with while there were Mulder; Adm. J.J. Johnson, head of South Africa's navy; Commo. D.K. Kinkead-Weekes, the naval operations director; and Maj. Gen. J.H. Robertze, the military's director of strategic studies.

In his *Esquire* article, Szulc wrote that "the Central Intelligence Agency and the South African secret services cooperate closely under the terms of a secret intelligence agreement, similar to United States intelligence accords with NATO governments."

Washington was not the only NATO member to establish direct contacts with the South African military. The October 6, 1975, issue of the German weekly *Der Spiegel* reported: "German military officers, in agreement with their counterparts in the North Atlantic Treaty Organization, particularly British and French officers, operate freely to establish close contacts with the military forces of the South African Republic. NATO considers a militarily strong South Africa useful in safeguarding the sea route around the Cape of Good Hope. . . . Despite the arms embargo imposed by the United Nations, Bonn is prepared to strengthen the defense capabilities of South Africa."

Filling Pretoria's Arsenal

Ignoring the UN ban imposed in 1963, NATO countries continued to sell arms and military equipment to Pretoria, helping it to attain a military might greater than the combined forces of most of Black-ruled Africa.

They also boosted Pretoria's efforts toward self-sufficiency in arms production. In *Race to Power: The Struggle for Southern Africa,* the Africa Research Group notes that "nearly all the NATO countries permit their corporations to invest in the South African armaments industry. They place no restrictions on the transfer of military know-how, including the sale to South Africa of blueprints and patents for military production. For example, the entire South African army and police force are equipped with NATO FN rifles, manufactured in South Africa under license from NATO. All these governments permit their citizens to accept jobs in the South African arms industry" (pp. 124-25).

In line with the Tar Baby policy, Washington sold millions of dollars' worth of "dual purpose" equipment—largely aircraft—to Pretoria. In 1970, the year Tar Baby was adopted, U.S. aircraft exports to South Africa were valued at over $25 million; a year later they had jumped to $70 million, and in 1972 they rose to $80 million. Between 1967 and 1972, the total was over $272 million. These "dual purpose" aircraft included Bell helicopters suitable for police or military operations and twin-engined Lear jets that could be outfitted for reconnaissance and certain combat missions. Also included were C-141 Starlifter and C-130 Hercules transport planes capable of ferrying troops and equipment for military purposes.

The South African Air Commandos, a paramilitary flying militia trained for counterinsurgency operations, use small American Pipers and Cessnas. Although the Air Commandos are technically "civilians," and therefore the sale of U.S. planes to them does not legally contravene the UN arms embargo, they nevertheless are part of Pretoria's "security planning."

Some sales are made directly to the South African military. Jennifer Davis, a member of the Southern Africa Committee and a research director of the Africa Fund of the American Committee on Africa, stated in hearings before the Senate Foreign Relations

Committee on July 24, 1975, that "both light aircraft such as Cessnas and heavy transport planes, such as the Lockheed Hercules C 130 have been provided directly to the South African Government for military use, long after the supposed imposition of an embargo in 1963. According to the International Institute for Strategic Studies there are now at least 7 C-130's operating in transport squadrons of the South African Airforce. Cessnas are used in a squadron assigned to the army, and in both the Reserve squadrons and the Air Commando squadrons." (The quotation is taken from an edited version in *Southern Africa* magazine, December 1975, p. 38.)

In addition, between 1967 and 1972 more than $22 million worth of communications equipment, including radar and electronic search and detection gear, was exported from the United States to South Africa. At least four IBM computers were supplied directly to the South African Department of Defense. In the same period about $10 million worth of herbicides and defoliants of the type used by Washington in Vietnam were sold to Pretoria. A General Motors plant built in South Africa was specifically designed to allow conversion to military production if necessary.

Until June 1975, London maintained a formal military pact with Pretoria in which it pledged to "defend" the sea route around the Cape of Good Hope in exchange for British naval use of the Simonstown base. According to the September 1975 *South African Scope*, "The Agreement made no specific mention of the supply of arms but the supply of arms was regarded by South Africa as a 'gentleman's agreement' between two allies." Although the Labour Party government in Britain had maintained a formal ban on arms sales to the Pretoria regime, it was reported in early 1975 to have agreed to license the sale of spare parts for British-built helicopters and Buccaneer aircraft. Under political pressure, London formally dissolved the Simonstown agreement, but indicated that British ships would continue to use the South African port on a "customer" basis.

The French government has been the most open in its sales of military equipment to the South Africans. Pretoria has more than forty French Mirage IIIs in fighter-bomber, interceptor, and reconnaissance versions, as well as four squadrons of Alouette helicopters and three Daphne-class French-built submarines. As of late 1975, forty-five Mirage F-1 jet fighters, the most advanced military aircraft built in France, were scheduled to be sent to

South Africa to replace the older Mirage IIIs. Paris also pledged to supply additional helicopters and two more submarines.

Pretoria is scheduled to start assembling its own F-1s by 1977. And Bernard Kaplan reported in the August 29, 1975, *Washington Post* that "South African engineers and designers are working long hours here [in Paris] with their counterparts at Dassault, the company which makes the F-1, on a program for South Africa to manufacture the plane from scratch."

Another joint project between France and South Africa was the financing and development of the Cactus (or Crotale) ground-to-air missile system. In 1972, Rockwell International, one of the largest American arms manufacturers, signed an agreement with the French electronics company Thomson-CSF to help produce the missile in South Africa if it was adopted by the U.S. Army.

In addition, Pretoria concluded deals with Spain for mortars and rockets and with Italy for torpedoes. South Africa began production of the Impala trainer—a light, jet-powered strike aircraft—under license from Italy in 1967; by 1973 it had built 200 of them.

The military equipment Pretoria obtained from its partners in NATO played a major part in its operations in Angola. An editorial in the December 19, 1975, *Le Monde* pointed out, "France, notably, cannot ignore the fact that the helicopters, mortars, machine guns, and other weapons used in the [Angola] conflict by South Africa were furnished by Paris or manufactured under French license." The January 8, 1976, issue of the Long Island, New York, paper *Newsday* reported that the South Africans used four C-141s, bought from the United States during the previous two years, to ferry troops and equipment to at least three sites within Angola.

By supplying South Africa with vast amounts of military equipment, the NATO powers are not only bolstering its ability to control the Cape sea route and combat internal "subversion." They are also equipping it to act as a powerful counterrevolutionary force throughout southern Africa, capable of furthering Western as well as South African political and economic interests. The intervention in Angola has been the most significant example so far.

While Pretoria's role in Angola was undoubtedly motivated to a large extent by its own particular interests, it was in full accord with the interests of the NATO powers, Washington in particular—and carried out with active American collaboration.

Senator Richard Clark revealed in January 1976 that Washington and Pretoria were exchanging intelligence information on the war in Angola. Sean Gervasi said at his December 19, 1975, press conference that, according to "high sources in the Defense Department," U.S. cargo planes were air-dropping supplies to South African columns operating in Angola.

A South African official cited by *New York Times* correspondent Henry Kamm in a February 5 dispatch from Cape Town indicated that Pretoria had actually received encouragement from Washington to go into Angola. The intervention, Kamm reported, was initiated "on the understanding that the United States would rush sufficient supplies to make it possible to counter the Soviet-supported movement." That understanding, the official added, had been based on contacts with American officials. "We had been in touch," he said. "We felt if we could give them a lapse of time they could find ways and means." Earlier in the interview the South African remarked, "We accepted the utterances of Mr. Kissinger and others. We felt surely he has the necessary pull to come forward with the goods."

South African Defense Minister Botha also alluded publicly to this U.S. collaboration. During a news conference in Cape Town on February 3, 1976, he declared that the South African intervention had the blessing of several African countries and at least one "free world" power. As quoted in the February 4 *Washington Post*, Botha refused to identify that power as Washington, stating, "I would be the last man to destroy our diplomatic relations with the United States." When asked about stories in the press that the CIA and the South African Bureau of State Security (BOSS) had arranged the intervention, Botha replied, "If it were so, it was not the only channel."

The Stakes for
South African Imperialism

Pretoria's military buildup, while it had been under way for a number of years, accelerated significantly after the April 1974 coup in Portugal, which opened the way for nationalist upsurges near South Africa's borders and deprived Pretoria of its strongest ally in southern Africa. The white rulers understood that the prospect of independence for Angola and Mozambique made it more difficult for them to prevent the spread of Black nationalist ideas within South Africa itself. The demonstrations in 1974 by Black students in Durban, in solidarity with the Mozambique independence fighters, was a clear signal of the dangers that lay ahead for the apartheid regime.

An official military circular declared in July 1974, "We are no longer preparing for war, we are at war." Defense Minister Pieter W. Botha said a few months later, "Our task is to prevent revolt and armed clashes." The entire South African army was reorganized into two main forces, a conventional military force and a counterinsurgency force. The military budget for the 1975-76 fiscal year reached a record $1.4 billion, twice the figure of two years before and more than 20 percent of the entire South African government budget. An additional $20 million was allocated for the Bureau of State Security (BOSS, the South African secret police) and $380 million for the regular police force and prison system.

Introducing the military budget on March 26, 1975, Minister of Finance Owen Horwood noted, "Although the government hope to achieve *detente* with black Africa, until it is achieved it is imperative to enable the defence forces to defend the republic's borders effectively." What Horwood meant by "defending" South Africa's borders became clearer several months later.

The South African intervention in Angola developed in two stages. The first began in August 1975 when South African forces occupied the construction sites for the hydroelectric dam project on the Cunene River in southern Angola. Simultaneously, they launched attacks against the Angolan bases of SWAPO—the South-West African People's Organisation—which has been resisting South Africa's occupation of Namibia (South-West Africa). The South African troops also clashed sporadically with MPLA and UNITA forces during these operations.

The second stage began in October, when Pretoria sent in additional forces to fight against the MPLA in alliance with the FNLA and UNITA.

The Cunene hydroelectric project was a cornerstone of Pretoria's efforts to increase its exploitation of Namibia's natural resources, which include large deposits of zinc, copper, uranium, and diamonds (the Oranjemund diamond mine is the largest in the world). Developed at a total cost of 188 million rand (about US$216 million), the Cunene dams and generating stations were to provide most of the power for the large mines in Namibia, as well as for some of the mining interests in southern Angola. However, under the agreement signed between Pretoria and the Portuguese colonialists in 1969, no power from the Cunene project was to be supplied to Angola during its first phase of operation and royalty payments to Angola were pegged at a low rate.

The November 1975 *African Development* described some of the fears that the South Africans had about the effects of the Angola crisis on the Cunene scheme: "It is now widely expected that the new leaders who emerge after November 11 will hold out for a higher royalty payment; it would even be possible for a hostile government in effective control of the area to cut off the flow of water from the Gove and Calueque dams. This could seriously disrupt production at the mines in Namibia, particularly at Rössing Uranium." The magazine also noted South African fears "of the influence by Angolan liberation movements and the South West African Peoples' Organisation over the African construction workers."

In its occupation of the Cunene facilities in August 1975, Pretoria had the full cooperation of the Portuguese military junta, which was still in formal control of Angola at the time. Replying to charges that South Africa had invaded Angola, Defense

Minister Botha revealed November 22 that the sending of troops to "protect" the Cunene installations had been carried out with the prior approval of Lisbon.

The War Against Namibia

Pretoria's war in Namibia was designed to maintain South African domination of the country, which dates back to 1915. In that year South Africa, as a participant in the First World War on the side of the Allies, drove the German colonialists out of Namibia and occupied the country. A few years later the League of Nations granted South Africa a mandate to administer Namibia as a "sacred trust of civilization." When the League of Nations was replaced by the United Nations after World War II, Pretoria refused to yield its mandate. In 1966 the UN revoked the mandate, declaring the continued South African occupation illegal. Pretoria ignored the ruling and tightened its control of the country. By 1969, virtually the entire governmental and economic apparatus of Namibia was being directly administered from Pretoria. South Africa's repressive laws and apartheid policies were also extended to Namibia.

Pretoria took advantage of the civil war in Angola to strike out at SWAPO bases just across the Namibian border. (The Ovambos, among whom SWAPO gets much of its support, straddle the border; about 400,000 live in Namibia and 100,000 in Angola. In addition, in mid-1975 many SWAPO supporters had fled into Angola to escape South African attacks.) The November 29, 1975, issue of the Cape Town daily *Die Burger*, an Afrikaans-language newspaper that serves as the official mouthpiece of the ruling National Party, carried a front-page article describing the attacks against SWAPO as part of a three-pronged South African intervention in Angola. The other two prongs were the occupation of the Cunene dam sites and the "joint struggle" with the FNLA and UNITA against the MPLA.

The newspaper also referred to the South African policy of "hot pursuit" against the Namibian rebels. "There is a lot of hot pursuit on the border," it said. "It does not need much imagination to see that a considerable clearing-up operation is being conducted there." Through news leaks to Western journalists, Pretoria made it known that it was ready to penetrate more than 200 miles into Angola to attack SWAPO guerrillas. *Die Burger* admitted that South African troops were effectively in occupation of part of Angola. Dozens of SWAPO rebels were reportedly killed and at least two bases destroyed in South African assaults carried out in October and November.

The South African incursions into southern Angola were also directed against the civilian population. According to a SWAPO press release issued in September, "South African military forces have now begun to strafe and attack villages and remote areas in southern Angola. . . . Now, recent Angolan refugees to Zambia tell of strikes into Angola by low-flying South African military aircraft."

The attacks against villages in southern Angola were accompanied by efforts in northern Namibia to isolate SWAPO guerrillas from their supporters. According to SWAPO administrative Secretary Moses Garoeb, who was quoted in the September 1975 issue of *Africa,* the regions of Ovamboland, Okavangoland, and Eastern Caprivi were placed under total South African military occupation. In some areas the inhabitants were herded into "protected villages" after their own villages were destroyed.

The War Against Angola

The first major South African intervention in the Angolan civil war began in late October 1975, at a time when the MPLA militarily occupied most of the cities along the Atlantic coast and was pressing the UNITA forces in the south. The South Africans provided logistical support for the Chipenda Brigade—which, although headed by Daniel Chipenda of the FNLA, included many white mercenaries in its ranks—and for the UNITA forces.

A South African–backed military column swept through southern and coastal Angola, taking in rapid succession the cities of Sá da Bandeira, Moçâmedes, Benguela, Lobito, and Novo Redondo. The November 17 *Der Spiegel* reported that the column was equipped with Alouette helicopters, Panhard armored cars, Marmon-Herrington light tanks, and 4.2-inch mortars—all of which are used in the South African army. The armored column reportedly received its supplies from South African bases in Namibia, as well as from a forward base set up at Sá da Bandeira.

In mid-November foreign correspondents in Angola confirmed the presence of South African soldiers. In a dispatch published in the November 16 London *Observer,* Tony Hodges reported:

I flew into Benguela on Monday [November 10], the day before Angola became formally independent from Portugal. Shortly after landing, we saw over 50 uniformed South African troops stacking arms crates in the airport hangars. Two Panhard armoured cars, manned by young, sandy-haired South African soldiers, guarded the airport access road. They were aged between 18 and 20, too young to be mercenaries.

A Japanese journalist and I were able to speak to three young, white soldiers at another UNITA-held town, Silva Porto, 250 miles east of here. Two were driving armoured cars daubed with "Viva UNITA" slogans.

They refused to disclose their nationality; but they could not understand Portuguese and spoke English with strong South African accents. We were not allowed to photograph them.

Reuters correspondent Fred Bridgland said in a report in the November 16 *Los Angeles Times:*

> In the past two weeks, I have spoken to white soldiers with South African accents in armored cars at Silva Porto, 425 miles north of Angola's border with the South African-administered territory of South-West Africa.
>
> I have also seen fair-skinned troops, many of them blond-haired, in the coastal cities of Benguela and Lobito, from which MPLA forces have retreated. . . .
>
> A Portuguese working closely with UNITA told me: "The South Africans are doing a good job. They are professionals.
>
> "This is their war. If they don't fight the war here now, they will have to fight it on their side."

Despite such eyewitness accounts—and the fact that South African troops were captured by the MPLA and presented to the press—Pretoria continued to issue official denials that its forces were involved in the civil war. However, South African newspapers, which are barred from printing unauthorized articles on military movements, began leaking information on Pretoria's role in Angola. Newspapers in Johannesburg carried reports November 16 of the existence of an airlift between the Rand airport, near Johannesburg, and Sá da Bandeira, flying into Angola "mercenaries, mainly of Portuguese nationality, but also South Africans and veteran mercenaries from the Congo."

The November 29 issue of Cape Town's *Die Burger* hinted that South African advisers were also active in the war: "It is no longer a bush war of a small resistance band. It is becoming a sort of conventional war of rapidly moving vehicle columns, artillery and projectiles. This requires know-how, leadership and planning on a level which is not readily available among Angola's black population."

U.S. intelligence sources cited by David Binder in the December 12 *New York Times* estimated that 1,000 South African troops were in Angola. However, *Washington Post* reporter David B. Ottaway said in the November 30 issue that sources in Lusaka placed the number at between 2,500 and 6,000 and said they were fighting simultaneously against the MPLA and the Namibian independence forces based in Angola.

The government-sanctioned leaks were accompanied by military moves that indicated plans for deeper involvement. Units along the Namibia-Angola border were strengthened, reserve officers were placed on alert, and Christmas leaves were canceled. In early January more than 15,000 South African males between the ages of seventeen and twenty-five were conscripted for a minimum of a year's military service. In addition, an undisclosed number of reservists were called up for three months of training. The conscription was one of the largest ever carried out in South Africa.

The November news leaks and preparations for stepped-up military intervention came mid reports that the South African-supported column had been stalled by the MPLA north of Novo Redondo. At the same time, South Africa launched a propaganda barrage against the Soviet and Cuban involvement, similar to the one emanating from Washington. Defense Minister Botha called on countries in the region, "separately and collectively," to act against Soviet plans to "subvert" southern Africa. The November 23 Johannesburg *Sunday Times* described Moscow's involvement in Angola as an attempt to gain "control of Africa."

In a major address on December 31, Prime Minister Vorster added his voice to this hysterical chorus. "It is obvious that South Africa is concerned over blatant Russian and Cuban intervention in Angola," he declared. "We are concerned because we know that the aim is not simply the establishment of a Marxist state in Angola, but to endeavor to create a whole row of Marxist states from Angola to Dar es Salaam and if it is at all possible, to divide Africa into two that way. . . . If they achieve their objective, not a single African country will be able to feel safe."

Foremost on Vorster's list of "endangered" countries, of course, was South Africa—or more specifically, the white supremacist regime. While Pretoria shared Washington's goal of preventing

Moscow from gaining strong political influence in an independent Angola, it did so from a more immediate perspective. Washington was primarily concerned with the effects Angola could have on the détente relationship with the Soviet Union. Pretoria feared that an MPLA regime, with Soviet backing, might provide greater support for the African nationalist groups of Namibia, Zimbabwe, and South Africa itself.

Pretoria, however, did not want to face the risks of a massive imperialist intervention in Angola alone. On November 27 Botha called for "more direct Free World action" to counter Moscow's involvement. Pretoria, he said, would "surely take part" in such a campaign. Vorster echoed this call in his December 31 speech, proclaiming that "only a bigger Western involvement, not only in the diplomatic but all other fields" could prevent Angola from being "hounded into the Communist fold." In addition to asking for a greater arms flow into Angola, Pretoria wanted the Western powers to become more open in their intervention, apparently as a sign of political backing for the South African role.

Although Pretoria had already greatly increased its military capability, the pleas for a stepped-up U.S. and European involvement indicated that it was still basically dependent on Western backing for any large-scale intervention beyond its borders. The ruling National Party expressed this through an article in the November 29 *Die Burger:* "If they [the Western powers] do not want to help out of fear of the Soviet Union, or if they want to wait and see, they cannot expect that South Africa will intensify its role so that in the end it is left carrying the baby alone."

Washington had given its encouragement to the initial South African intervention and showed its willingness to pour in arms shipments and mercenaries—if not American troops themselves—to achieve its aims in Angola and back up the South African forces. But the antiwar sentiment of the American population, together with the pressure which that sentiment placed on Congress, greatly limited Washington's ability to proceed with its interventionist plans. That, in turn, had an important effect on the extent of South Africa's involvement in Angola.

Pretoria expressed sharp disappointment with the December 19 Senate vote that cut off arms aid to the FNLA and UNITA. A December 31 *Washington Post* dispatch from Johannesburg reported that a South African radio commentator, who generally reflected the views of official circles, said, "Angola was the testing-ground for the will of the West to resist Soviet expansionism in Africa, and the American Senate has lost the first round." Less than a month later, South African troops pulled back from their positions along the battle fronts of south-central Angola. However, they were still in occupation of the Cunene installations. Pretoria indicated they would continue to halt "terrorist" actions launched into Namibia from southern Angola, and warned that South African units remained on alert in "nonoperational" areas.

Pretoria's Warning to Africa

An additional factor that influenced Pretoria's decision to intervene in Angola was the possible effect of the Angolan civil war on the South African regime's drive to establish a "détente" with Black Africa. Pretoria's principal aim in launching this "détente" policy was to enlist the cooperation of bourgeois African leaders, such as Kenneth Kaunda of Zambia, in curbing the activities of Black nationalist guerrillas based in their countries and defusing the potentially explosive conflict in Zimbabwe (Rhodesia).

Since late 1974, Kaunda and Vorster had cooperated closely in an effort to engineer a "political solution" to the crisis in Zimbabwe. Vorster put pressure on Rhodesian Prime Minister Ian Smith to make a few compromises with Zimbabwean nationalist leaders, while Kaunda arrested and harassed those Zimbabweans based in Zambia who were unwilling to accept a settlement that fell short of granting immediate majority rule. As with Angola, Pretoria's primary concern with the Zimbabwean struggle was the potential effect it could have on the Black population of South Africa. In addition, Pretoria sought to expand its trade and investment opportunities in the rest of the African continent.

The Angolan civil war threatened to upset Pretoria's "détente" schemes. Reporter Stanley Uys commented in a dispatch published in the January 15, 1976, *Washington Post* that, among official circles in Pretoria,

> there is anxiety, too, over the effect that control of Angola by the Popular Movement could have on two of South Africa's detente partners, President Kenneth Kaunda of Zambia and President Mobutu Sese Seko of Zaire.

Both Zambia and Zaire are experiencing serious financial problems, caused partly by the closing of the railway line that runs between the port of Benguela and Teixeira de Sousa in eastern Angola, and it is feared that this economic instability could ripple out into political instability. . . .

The anxiety that nags in Pretoria is that either Mobutu and Kaunda could be overthrown because of their "moderate" attitude toward South Africa, or that they could extricate themselves from detente . . . to protect their positions.

In October 1975, Pretoria may have calculated that by striking quickly into Angola it could tip the balance in favor of the UNITA and FNLA. UNITA leader Savimbi had already expressed his willingness to go along with the "détente" scheme several months earlier. In an interview in the April 28, 1975, Luanda *Portuguese Africa,* Savimbi declared that "economic cooperation with South Africa is only realism, however much we may be opposed to the inhumanity and injustice of apartheid." The May 2 issue of the same publication reported that "Dr Savimbi said he was in favour of detente and of dialogue as a means of solving problems, and that he did not believe, in the present Southern African context, that armed liberation wars were necessarily the solution for the problems of Namibia and Zimbabwe." Savimbi then went on to describe Vorster as a "responsible leader."

Perhaps one of the most ominous aspects of the South African intervention in Angola was its message to Blacks in Africa as a whole and particularly in southern Africa. By brandishing its military might, Pretoria was saying in effect that it would intervene anywhere it felt its interests were threatened. Pretoria was also pressuring the Black African regimes into going along with its "détente" scheme by presenting armed conflict with militarized South Africa as the only alternative. In case this warning was not understood by everyone, Defense Minister Botha spelled it out in a January 26, 1976, speech before the South African Parliament: "In the past we hit back with small forces. If necessary, we will retaliate with greater force."

While the danger to the African masses from Pretoria is a serious one in its own right, it cannot be separated from the shadow of Washington, the main bastion of imperialism and racism on a world scale. The American aggression in Angola— side by side with its South African ally—shows that the U.S. rulers are just as eager to intervene against struggles for self-determination in Africa as they are anywhere else in the world. Washington's long and brutal war against the Vietnamese people was an example of how far it is willing to go to protect its imperialist interests. The intervention in Angola has revealed that its basic strategy has not changed.

If not halted in time, Washington could plunge Angola—or any other African country—into a bloodbath like the one it carried out in Southeast Asia.

Part II

The American People and the Angolan Freedom Struggle

[The following is a report given by Tony Thomas to the Socialist Workers Party's National Committee, January 3, 1976, in Milwaukee.]

The Political Committee has proposed that we launch a national campaign against U.S. imperialist involvement in Angola. We want to help stop the intervention of the State Department, the CIA, and the Pentagon in the Angolan civil war. We want to help bring the secret moves of the Ford administration into the open and compel Kissinger and his cohorts to disclose the whole truth about their covert operations in Angola.

The American people as a whole are worried. They are pressing for an answer to the question: "Is Angola to become another Vietnam?" The question is being argued on a broad scale. This is a debate in which we are already involved. We propose a response like the one given during the Indochina war—a broad campaign of mobilization and propaganda around the slogan, "U.S. out of Angola. Not one penny, not one bullet, not a single adviser or soldier, into Angola."

We should not underestimate the danger of American military intervention, despite Kissinger's pledges not to commit U.S. troops. The American Committee on Africa reported on December 19, 1975, that American soldiers are being approached by officers at various bases to resign and sign up as mercenaries for the FNLA and UNITA. The committee also disclosed that American air force units have been put on alert to fly tactical air strikes in defense of South African troops in Angola, should the situation require it.

The propagandists of the Ford administration repeat the same line used to justify intervention in the Vietnamese civil war. They point to the alleged threat of a "Communist take-over." They remain silent about the four centuries of Portuguese imperialist domination. They remain silent about Washington's long-term policy of active support to Portugal's war against the right of the Angolan peoples to determine their own fate.

In the ten years before the rebellion in Angola erupted in 1961, Washington gave $298 million to Lisbon in military aid. In some years during this period the United States provided more than half the Portuguese military budget.

After the Angolans began fighting for their freedom in a way reminiscent of the American colonists of 1776, Washington continued to help the Portuguese. Portuguese officers and troops were trained at American military installations, including the Green Beret base at Fort Bragg.

During the last years of Portuguese colonial domination, American imperialism increased its support to Portugal against the African rebels.

Tad Szulc, formerly a correspondent of the *New York Times,* described the policy toward southern Africa laid down by Kissinger in 1970: "In a National Security Decision Memorandum secretly issued by the NSC [National Security Council] in January 1970, the administration set forth a new policy of 'communication' with white regimes in southern Africa (including Portugal as the ruling power in Angola and Mozambique) on the grounds that 'the whites are here to stay and the only way that constructive change can come about is through them' and that 'there is no hope for the blacks to gain the political rights they seek through violence, which will lead only to chaos and increased opportunities for the Communists.'"

Wall Street's interest in Angola centers on its resources. Angola is the third-largest coffee producer in the world. Much of its production goes to the United States. Diamond mines owned by American, South African, Belgian, and Portuguese interests produced more than two million carats in 1972 alone, with an export value of some $110 million. The country has important deposits of iron ore, manganese, phosphates, copper, granite, marble, and asphalt.

Most importantly, Angola has oil. Gulf Oil's concession in Cabinda produces about 10 million tons a year. By the turn of the century, Gulf projects pumping out more than 100 million tons a year from these fields alone. Exxon, Texaco, and the French Total corporation are exploring for oil in other parts of Angola.

In the Cunene River Valley in southern Angola, a large

hydroelectric power plant has been built by South African and Portuguese capital. In the next few years the source is scheduled to provide the bulk of the power needs for Namibia as well as Angola.

Other known resources remain largely untapped.

Angola's geographic location gives it important strategic value. It is in a position to control the mouth of the Congo River; and it borders on territories occupied by South Africa. Zambia and Zaïre depend on Angolan railroads and ports to ship their copper to world markets.

Moreover, Angolan events influence the affairs of Zambia, Zaïre, the People's Republic of Congo (Brazzaville), and the South African colony of Namibia in a direct as well as indirect way. Many of the ethnic groups or nationalities in Angola extend beyond the boundaries between these countries, which were drawn by the European colonial powers.

Angola's Independence Struggle

Despite the help given by American imperialism to Portuguese colonialism, the liberation struggle led by the Angolan National Liberation Front, the National Union for the Total Independence of Angola, the People's Movement for the Liberation of Angola, and the fighters in Guinea-Bissau and Mozambique eventually broke the Portuguese grip.

The armed actions began in 1961. The main ones took place in northern Angola where fighters of the Angolan Peoples' Union, led by Holden Roberto, initiated an uprising. The forces involved in this revolt were able to secure control over an area reaching 200 miles from the Congo (now Zaïre) border.

Portugal's response was the use of terror not only in the northern region but in Luanda and elsewhere. As many as one million people were forced to flee into Zaïre, Congo (Brazzaville), and Zambia.

Until the mid-1960s, it was the FNLA that carried out the main military actions in Angola. This is contrary to some of the claims of the MPLA and its supporters that the FNLA never fought as a real national liberation group and that only the MPLA was committed to the armed conflict. In fact, the FNLA played such a prominent role that the Fourth International in 1964 correctly recognized that the FNLA was leading the struggle at that time and should be supported accordingly against Portuguese imperialism. The Fourth International, of course, did not support the FNLA *politically,* for its program was not a revolutionary socialist one.

At the same time, the FNLA was slandered by the MPLA, which called it a tool of Western imperialism and of Tshombe's regime in the Congo. The truth was that Tshombe, who was backed by Portugal, Belgium, and Washington, severely harassed the FNLA. The Fourth International defended the FNLA against these slanders. Articles written by Livio Maitan, for example, pointed out that even if the FNLA had sought aid from Washington, what was essential was not such links but how the struggle of the Angolan masses for independence was carried on.

During this period, the MPLA was very weak—in 1963 it came close to dissolving. It lacked links with the fighters in Angola and with the refugees in Zaïre. However, in subsequent years it established links with Mbundu religious (Methodist) and ethnic leaders in north-central Angola. By 1967 it was able to gain bases in Zambia and Congo (Brazzaville), carrying out actions against the Portuguese in the areas bordering these countries.

The UNITA entered the field in 1965 and 1966. It began as a split from the FNLA led by Jonas Savimbi, who was the foreign affairs minister of the FNLA. The UNITA was joined by splitters from the MPLA who attacked that organization as "tribalistic" and "pro-Soviet." During the late 1960s and the early 1970s, the UNITA claimed to have no support from any foreign state. It said that all its activities were based inside Angola. At that time, the MPLA and the FNLA had headquarters abroad but carried out some activities within Angola.

The areas liberated by the UNITA were in south-central Angola, which is inhabited chiefly by the Ovimbundu people.

The inability of Portugal to continue the burden of the colonial wars was decisive in bringing about an end to the Salazar-Caetano regime and in touching off the mass struggles that have shaken Portugal since April 1974. The Portuguese imperialists sought to prop up various neocolonialist and white-settler organizations so as to postpone granting independence. All three liberation groups opposed this neocolonialist scheme and demanded immediate independence. All three, especially the FNLA, stepped up their guerrilla actions against the Portuguese.

On May 26, 1974, right after the downfall of Caetano, 20,000 Blacks demonstrated in Luanda, demanding independence. On July 15, in response to racist attacks on African communities, a general strike was staged, followed by occupations of universities and high schools by students, faculties, and staffs. This upsurge brought the Angolan working class into the political arena.

With the growth of non-Portuguese imperialist investments in the 1960s and 1970s, the working class expanded in Angola. In 1973, out of an African population of five to six million persons, there were 130,000 workers employed in manufacturing, mainly concentrated in Luanda, Lobito, and Nova Lisboa.

In the wave of mass actions in Angola following the April 1974 coup in Portugal, the workers in Luanda, Lobito, Benguela, and Nova Lisboa launched a wave of strikes for better pay and working conditions and against racist moves. In marches and demonstrations, participants carried the banners of each of the liberation groups.

To meet the problems posed by this wave of mass mobilization and workers' struggles, the Portuguese signed an agreement that brought the UNITA, the FNLA, and the MPLA into a so-called transitional government with Portuguese officials. Independence was to come later, following elections.

The establishment of the transitional government coincided with the opening of a new phase in the struggle. This phase has been marked by the breakup of the Portuguese colonial hold over Angola, by the efforts of the masses to establish their own government, and by the struggle of the various imperialist powers and other forces to gain control over the situation, or at least to take advantage of it.

The outstanding feature of this period has been the Angolan civil war—that is, the fighting between the three nationalist factions. This fratricidal conflict has greatly facilitated imperialist intervention. One of the aims of Washington, for instance, has been to deepen and exacerbate the hostilities.

Most of the groupings on the left have offered support to one or another of the nationalist factions in Angola against the others. Some of the Maoists support the FNLA or the UNITA; the pro-Moscow Stalinists, the group around the *Guardian* in the United States, and most of the ultraleft groups support the MPLA.

This is a question that is currently in dispute within the world Trotskyist movement. The International Majority Tendency (IMT) within the Fourth International favors supporting the MPLA. Their position has been presented most vigorously by C. Gabriel in an article "On the Question of Angola" published in the December 8, 1975, issue of *Intercontinental Press*. The leadership of the Partido Socialista de los Trabajadores in Argentina agrees with the IMT on this.

Those who agree with this position argue that in Angola the MPLA is supported by the working class and that because of this the MPLA must be supported no matter how inadequate or wrong its program may be. They contend that the MPLA must be credited with leading the workers' upsurge and that the victory of the FNLA and UNITA would signify the suppression and even massacre of the most radical wing of the workers. They also claim that the MPLA is more progressive than the other groups and has enacted a more progressive social program in the territories it controls. They further argue that the FNLA and the UNITA are not legitimate national liberation movements, but are venal agencies of Washington and other imperialist powers. The FNLA and UNITA are pictured as "tribalistic," that is, based on ethnic groups. The implication is that "tribalistic" types are more "backward" than the MPLA, which is pictured as a "pan-Angolan" movement.

The reality is somewhat different from that. So I'd like to take time to show how false and misleading this picture is.

The Character of the Nationalist Groupings

I think the issue that most of the supporters of the MPLA fail to weigh properly is the national question—what they choose to call "tribalism."

The MPLA, UNITA, and FNLA all claim to represent a "pan-Angolan" movement; and each of them pictures the two others as "tribalistic." The truth is that each of them is based on one of the country's three main ethnic groups.

With the exception of small urbanized layers, it is false to claim that an Angolan nationality exists in anything like finished form. The bulk of the population of Angola consists of ethnic groupings in well-defined geographical regions, spilling over into other countries in some cases. These groups have their own distinct languages and cultures, and they have their own body of historical experience as distinct peoples. In short, each of the three has the attributes of a nationality.

Angola's boundaries, after all, were determined by imperialist colonial powers, and not by the ethnic boundaries or the desires of the African masses. Also, Portuguese capitalism blocked the economic and political integration of the various Angolan peoples.

The liberation struggle developed unevenly, with each of the three groups representing one of the three main nationalities in the country. The MPLA's base is the Mbundu who live in north-central Angola and around Luanda. They number roughly one to one and a half million. The FNLA is based among the one to one and a half million Bakongos in the northwestern area of Angola. The UNITA finds its support among the more than two million Ovimbundu who inhabit the central region and southern Angola.

In fact, except for a few brief periods, the military positions of the groups have reflected the divisions of these different ethnic areas.

Ethnic divisions are also to be found in the urban areas. For example, in Lobito, the second most important port city, tens of thousands of demonstrators greeted the arrival of Jonas Savimbi and the UNITA when they took the town in November 1975. Not surprisingly, Lobito is a center for the Ovimbundu.

When the MPLA secured control of Luanda, their own newspapers reported that for days thousands of workers of Bakongo and Ovimbundu origin demonstrated, demanding transportation to FNLA- or UNITA-held areas. Thousands were able to get away to Lobito where they were met by pro-UNITA demonstrations. We have to anticipate that the victory of either side in this civil war may mean pogroms, with victims running into the tens of thousands. Each of the groups—not just the MPLA—is using the animosities among the nationalities to further its goals.

We must make it clear that we aren't exactly "Angolan patriots." Being a "pan-Angolan" is not necessarily more progressive than being for helping the Bakongo, the Ovimbundu, and the Mbundu establish working relations against the common enemy—imperialism.

As Leninists we understand that the road to uniting the masses in Angola against exploitation and oppression is not to denounce the national aspirations of the different Angolan peoples as "backward tribalism," but to support their right to self-determination, which includes the right to autonomy or even secession.

Urging a victory for one of these nationalist factions against the two others leads to exacerbating the tensions. The MPLA Central Committee, for example, has enacted a law which, in effect, denies Angolan citizenship to anyone collaborating with the FNLA and UNITA, a threat that is bound to strengthen their determination to fight to the death against an MPLA victory.

One reason why none of these groups has really cut across the lines of nationality is that they stand on procapitalist and anti-working class social and economic programs that are basically similar. That was also one of the reasons why the Portuguese brought the nationalist groups into the transitional government. The Portuguese wanted to use them to curb the working class upsurge.

This goes counter to the arguments pushed by supporters of the MPLA who claim that the MPLA is more "progressive" than the UNITA or the FNLA, or at least more sensitive to pressures from the working class.

All three groups collaborated with the Portuguese during the coalition government established in January 1975. Particularly active in controlling the working class were the UNITA and the MPLA, which are supported in the urban centers.

One of the first measures these groups took was to appeal to the workers to stop their strikes. The appeal was soon followed by a decree empowering the government to place striking dockers and other workers under military control.

The three groups tried to use the antistrike campaign to gain factional advantages, as well as to try to maintain their bases among the workers. For example, when the dockers in Lobito struck, the MPLA used this as an excuse to send troops against the UNITA. The MPLA claimed that UNITA troops were responsible for the strike, since the dockers were Ovimbundu supporters of the UNITA.

This is not to say that the UNITA played a more progressive role in that situation. After the MPLA attack on the strikers was beaten back, the UNITA helped break the strike by claiming that the dockers were blocking Zambian supplies for African liberation forces.

Since the collapse of the coalition regime and the initiation of civil war in July 1975, there has been no change in the attitude of these groups, including the MPLA, toward the workers.

In Luanda, under MPLA control, harbor work has been returned to almost around the clock, hours having been lengthened with no pay increases. There may be some labor resistance there, judging from the continual denunciations by MPLA leaders of workers who do not comply with the speedup as "saboteurs".

Another indication is the report that a crackdown on working class militants took place recently in Luanda. This followed an earlier report of a purge of "left-wing" members of the MPLA.

The recent arrests of militants occurred in the context of a witch-hunt in Luanda against "Trotskyism" even though there is no indication that a large, or even any, Trotskyist group exists in the country. Supporters of the Fourth International in Portugal have reported that Angolan students interested in Trotskyism, who returned to MPLA areas, were driven out by the MPLA at gunpoint.

On the crucial question of the working class upsurge the facts show that the MPLA has taken the same basic stand as the FNLA and UNITA. The MPLA aims to break strikes, lengthen hours, and block independent organization of political action by the working class.

One claim made by the IMT is that the MPLA is supported by the most radical layers of the working class, who would be suppressed if the other groups entered Luanda. Even if this were true, it could be argued just as cogently that with an MPLA victory in Lobito, the MPLA would suppress the pro-UNITA working class militants such as the dockers against whom the MPLA sent troops.

Whatever support the MPLA may have obtained from the working class in the Mbundu areas, it has already broken strikes and arrested working class militants in Luanda, and suppressed expressions of real working class political radicalism.

The class lines in Angola do not follow ethnic lines but exist between the workers and the leaderships of all three nationalist factions. The indicated course for the workers and their allies, in Luanda, Lobito, the Bakongo, Mbundu, and Ovimbundu areas, and all other parts of Angola, is to press ahead independently.

The workers and their allies need to break from each of these groups and form a party of their own based on a revolutionary working class program.

Only by following that kind of program can the workers cut across the factional divisions and national animosities feeding the civil war. A program of class independence is required by the Angolan working masses to defeat the anti–working class policies of the three nationalist groups and their neocolonialist and imperialist backers.

Still another element in the situation is the imperialist support given to the UNITA and the FNLA, including the use of South African troops. Does this automatically require us to support the MPLA?

First of all we have to consider our criteria. If we put a plus wherever the White House puts a minus, or if we put a minus wherever the White House puts a plus, it would be very simple to determine our policies.

This question came up for discussion in a different context last summer in the Fourth International in relation to the Portuguese Socialist Party's defense of its democratic rights. Should we have opposed this defense because the CIA channeled funds to the SP and because Wall Street's propagandists claimed they were defending democracy by favoring the SP over the Communist Party? We answered no—although we of course sharply opposed the class-collaborationist, counterrevolutionary policies of the Portuguese SP.

In Angola we must begin by checking the stands of the three groups in relation to imperialism. Here again we find no basic difference. The MPLA has made it very clear—as have the UNITA and the FNLA—that it favors foreign imperialist investments in Angola. In fact, while they participated in the transitional government, the nationalist groups found themselves in mutual accord in this respect. All three favored continued foreign investment, with the proviso that in major resource industries the government should hold 51 percent of the ownership.

The government already held a 51 percent share of Gulf Oil's concession in Cabinda and a similar share in the diamond concession owned by South African, Belgian, Portuguese, and American interests.

Moreover, many of the Portuguese holdings had already been nationalized owing to MFA (Armed Forces Movement) decisions in Portugal. The only major action of this kind that was demanded, particularly by the MPLA and the FNLA, was expropriation of the coffee plantations and farms. On this point there was joint agreement, a consensus that was reached without great difficulty since most of the smaller Portuguese coffee planters had already fled Angola.

In addition, each of the groups has shown its willingness to solicit imperialist political, material—and even military—support against its enemies.

The MPLA, for example, solicited the support of the MFA

regime while it still governed Angola. Although the Portuguese rulers were divided on how to respond, their main line after the transitional government was set up tended to be in support of the MPLA. For example, when the MPLA forced the FNLA and UNITA out of Luanda, the Portuguese army announced that it would prevent any attempt by the FNLA to return to the city. The MPLA received thousands of rifles, plus trucks, ships, and other equipment when the Portuguese withdrew from Angola, while most of this type of equipment was withdrawn from UNITA and FNLA areas (some of which was taken to MPLA areas).

The MPLA also has sought, and boasts of having received, material and political support from the governments of the smaller imperialist powers such as the Scandinavian countries, Holland, Belgium, and Canada. This support may have declined in recent months because of U.S. pressure.

We should add that the MPLA has maintained good relations with some of the biggest imperialist companies holding concessions in its territories—even those whose governments are actively supporting the UNITA or the FNLA.

Gulf Oil holds the biggest imperialist concession in Angola, grossing more than $1 billion a year from its Cabinda wells, which are to be stepped up to ten times their current output in a few years. There are many reports from the MPLA, from the U.S. State Department, and from sources in Gulf Oil, that relations between the MPLA and Gulf Oil are very good. There have even been reports that Gulf is trying to put pressure on the State Department to change its current anti-MPLA line.

Gulf Oil was the main financial stay of the MPLA until December 22, 1975, when the State Department forced the company to suspend payments. In September and October Gulf Oil gave $116 million to the MPLA. It planned to make another $95 million payment by December 31. However, after Acting Assistant Secretary of State for African Affairs Edward Mulcahy put the squeeze on Gulf Oil, the company halted payments.

The September-October payment was three times the reported U.S. aid to the FNLA and UNITA combined. It matched the reported Soviet aid to the MPLA for the entire year of 1975. Thus from the formal point of who is on the receiving end of American imperialist aid—the MPLA was the recipient of the most American aid until a few weeks ago. Of course, the aid did not come from the Ford administration but from the biggest imperialist company operating in the country.

The stopping of payments for the time being came after a battle between the State Department and Gulf Oil. Gulf had tried to induce the State Department to take a less truculent stand toward the MPLA. Kissinger was strong enough to win this battle. The contest is indicative of the divisions in the American ruling class over intervention in Angola.

The friendly relations between Gulf Oil and the MPLA are not unique. Other companies of the same type get similar treatment.

This does not prove that the MPLA is controlled by Gulf Oil. It only underlines the point that each of these nationalist organizations holds an identical position toward imperialism; each of them maneuvers with imperialism; each is willing to make political and economic concessions to gain imperialist support.

The groups are real nationalist movements with mass support; consequently they are not mere puppets of imperialism. It is their factional rivalry, deepened now to the level of a civil war, that has exacerbated their readiness to invite aid from abroad to match their opponents in heavy arms and sophisticated military equipment.

To seek imperialist aid is common among such nationalist groups. Moreover, the various imperialist forces often intervene— as in this situation—on several sides to make sure that their interests are preserved no matter who wins.

It may be that the main strategy of the State Department in the current conflict is not to tip the scales decisively in favor of one of the sides—which could easily have been done by sending more massive aid to the UNITA and the FNLA or by more massive involvement of South African troops. The State Department may be aiming at maintaining a balance of power between the three groups, preventing the total defeat of the UNITA and the FNLA. As time goes on, the Angolan masses may become exhausted and each faction will become more receptive to attempts by imperialism to increase its influence in return for support.

Kissinger gives as one of his reasons for supporting the FNLA and UNITA the intervention of the Kremlin in the Angolan situation on the side of the MPLA. Moscow granted an estimated $100 million worth of military supplies to the MPLA during 1975.

The Kremlin's aims are the same as in other colonial and semicolonial areas. It seeks to strengthen the diplomatic influence of the Soviet Union, but without extending the world revolution or really assisting the national liberation of Angola.

In fact, like Washington, Moscow does not appear to be aiming to bring about a total victory for the side it favors. The Soviet bureaucrats are looking for chips to be used for bargaining purposes within the context of "détente" with American imperialism. That is the basis of the Kremlin's approach to the MPLA.

Another objective is to counteract Peking's prestige in Africa. By backing a supposedly progressive MPLA, pitted against the UNITA and the FNLA, which have received support from China, Moscow's image can be enhanced at the expense of Peking. In Africa, Moscow has long been regarded with less sympathy than Peking. In fact, Guinea-Bissau and Mozambique, two countries whose leaders are closely aligned with the MPLA, have closer relations with Peking than with Moscow.

The intervention of Cuba, which is reported to have as many as 5,000 troops in Angola, is subsidiary to the involvement of the Soviet Union. For diplomatic reasons, Moscow prefers not to send Soviet troops. From the Cuban viewpoint, the action may be considered worthwhile as a demonstration of opposition to imperialism.

Kissinger has denounced Moscow's support of the MPLA, claiming that this puts in question the détente as a whole. At the same time, Kissinger has not proposed any serious countermoves such as cutting off grain sales to the Soviet Union. But even if this propaganda were to be taken at face value, does this mean that we should support the "right" of a workers' state to take advantage of a situation like the one in Angola and that this calls for giving political support to the MPLA?

We don't think so. The interests of the world revolution do not coincide with the interests of the parasitic Soviet bureaucracy or its narrow diplomatic maneuvers. The military and diplomatic support given by the Kremlin to the MPLA is not meant to help the Angolan masses but to place the MPLA regime under obligations to Moscow.

If we were to base our stand on the actions of the representatives of a bureaucratized workers' state, we would face a difficulty.

North Korea and China have sent advisers and some military aid to the FNLA and the UNITA. Romania, another bureaucratized workers' state, has pursued a policy of courting and aiding all sides in the current conflict. So which camp do we choose among these workers' states that are fishing in the troubled waters of Angola?

Do we believe that Cuba and the Soviet Union are more "progressive" in supporting one petty-bourgeois nationalist faction than Peking and Pyongyang are in supporting a different petty-bourgeois nationalist faction?

If no confidence can be placed in the capacity of any of the factions to advance the socialist revolution in Angola or on an international scale, it follows that the aid offered by the bureaucracy of a degenerated or deformed workers' state will not change that political conclusion.

For example, the counterrevolutionary bureaucrats who run the Soviet Union aren't at all opposed to the strikebreaking or the arrests of militants—especially under the cover of a witch-hunt against "Trotskyism." In fact, they may have made such a witch-hunt one of the conditions of their aid to the MPLA.

It is clear that a revolutionary-Marxist position in the Angolan civil war cannot be automatically derived from the Soviet and Cuban intervention in behalf of the MPLA, or from the Chinese and North Korean intervention in behalf of the UNITA or the FNLA.

The civil war involves basically three unprincipled nationalist factions that follow procapitalist, anti–working class and class-collaborationist policies.

South Africa's Intervention

The most ominous development in the Angolan civil war is the intervention of South Africa. This is one of the consequences of the unprincipled character of the contestants, who invite foreign intervention, no matter how reactionary its nature.

The South African intervention has passed through several phases. The initial South African incursions began in late June or July 1975. Their immediate objective was the pursuit of SWAPO (South West African People's Organisation) guerrillas from Namibia who had crossed the border into Angola. South African troops had been barred from such forays under Portuguese rule, even under the Salazar-Caetano dictatorship. The Portuguese feared that South African incursions would pave the way for South African penetration of the area.

The pursuit of SWAPO guerrillas was followed in August by seizure of the Cunene dam and military occupation of the area.

It is important to note that the FNLA and UNITA did not serve as puppets of South Africa in this imperialist incursion. The

FNLA publicly denounced the South African intervention, and the UNITA and the MPLA, which had forces in the area, put up some resistance.

It was the deepening civil war that prevented the three organizations from joining forces and driving the South African forces out of Angola.

In October, reports began to appear in the press that South African troops were involved in a drive of UNITA and FNLA forces up the coast from the South. According to the MPLA, the column included several hundred South African troops, some of whom were masquerading as mercenaries. Other sources claim that today five or six thousand South African troops have intervened in Angola with more troops being stationed in the border areas of Namibia.

Because of the South African censorship and the efforts of the FNLA and UNITA to cover up the South African moves, it is not clear at the moment which field of operations is primary, pursuit of SWAPO, occupation of the Cunene valley, or military thrusts against the MPLA.

The South Africans have intervened for four obvious reasons: 1) to maintain control over the Cunene region; 2) to strengthen their grip on Namibia; 3) to tip the balance in the civil war toward the UNITA and the FNLA; 4) to facilitate the counter-revolutionary designs of the U.S. State Department.

The UNITA and FNLA must be condemned for blocking with the South Africans, just as the MPLA had to be condemned for collaborating with the Portuguese colonial army against the FNLA and UNITA.

As for the Vorster regime in South Africa, it must be pilloried along with the Ford administration for intervening in the Angolan civil war. Vorster is using South African troops to help pave the way for use of troops from other imperialist powers. Our slogan must be "South Africa out of Angola!"

What Position for Revolutionaries?

Our judgment of the civil war between the nationalist groups in Angola can be summarized as follows: 1) All three of these groups favor collaboration with imperialism and are opposed to working class mobilization and any real struggle for socialism. 2) All three of them seek to inflame animosities between the main nationalities in Angola. 3) At the same time each of them has a real mass base and has played a real role in the struggle for independence.

In our opinion, no political support ought to be given to any of these three nationalist groups. The victory of any one of the three offers no special promise of advancing the Angolan masses toward socialism or toward greater independence from imperialism. To impose the domination of one nationality over the other two nationalities offers no stable solution to the problems facing Angola and would only facilitate imperialist designs on the country.

In fact, I do not think that any of these groups can "win" the struggle in view of the broad popular base each has. If one of them does gain a decisive victory over the others, its current political outlook could signify a repression in which the real winner would be imperialism.

Our position is one of opposition to the factional war. We stand for the program of socialism—for the struggles of the workers, the youth, and the peasants that point toward a socialist society. We are opposed to the program and practices of each of the nationalist groups. We are for a class-struggle policy for the masses.

Our job as American revolutionary socialists is to oppose imperialist intervention in Angola, particularly American imperialist intervention. Our job is to build meetings, organize picket lines and demonstrations, and do everything possible to deepen the opposition that already exists against intervention in the Angolan civil war.

If the imperialist intervention increases, as seems quite likely, we may decide to favor the victory of one or another of the groups on tactical grounds. If, for example, the war becomes basically a war for national liberation against an imperialist invasion, we will favor the defeat of the imperialists, the victory of whatever groups oppose the imperialists, and the defeat of any groups that become imperialist puppets.

However, as I have indicated, it would not be correct for us to take such a stand at this point. Our main concern is to mount an effective campaign against Washington's intervention in the civil war and against its aim of blocking the national liberation and social struggles of the Angolan peoples.

[Following the report there was extensive discussion by committee members, after which the reporter summarized.]

Concluding Remarks

I would like to begin by taking up a few of the factual questions raised during the discussion. I think it is important to realize that many of these factual questions are very hard to answer, as Fred Halstead pointed out. We try to go by concrete information: things that have been verified, usually even by pro-MPLA sources, such as many of the newspapers in Portugal, many of the publications in Angola published by the MPLA itself, as well as the reports of comrades who have been able to go to Angola.

Our statements on the slanders of the MPLA against the FNLA are not something recent. This was the position of the Fourth International throughout the initial years of the struggle. Only in the last couple of years did the International Majority Tendency make a shift on this.

It is rather dangerous to make flat, unqualified statements about one group favoring imperialism while another does not, or about one group not being a real national liberation movement while a different one is. The concrete facts have to be taken into consideration. The facts show that the other two groups are not simply imperialist puppets, despite the assertions of the MPLA. It is not a matter of an Angolan Ky or Thieu or somebody like Ngo Dinh Diem, who was brought over to Vietnam from New Jersey. The analogy with Vietnam in this respect does not hold.

The FNLA and UNITA are real movements, real movements that have proven many times over that they have mass support. Even the MPLA says that it has no hope of politically winning over the people in regions like the Bakongo. And those areas are not just tiny pockets. Each liberation group has roughly a quarter to a third of the support in Angola.

I think it is important to emphasize some of the points that Sam Manuel made. What do the three groups stand for? On the basic question of their attitude toward imperialism there is no fundamental difference.

One speaker mentioned that the MPLA does not call for a mass campaign against U.S. imperialism—perhaps because the MPLA does not want to disrupt détente. The MPLA's attitude is not primarily related to the détente between Moscow and Washington. It is true that the MPLA does not call for a big mass campaign against American imperialism. But that's not because of concern about the détente. They are looking ahead and holding open the possibility of friendly relations with American imperialism. This is the counterpart of the policy of the other two groups, who have been trying to outbid the MPLA in seeking friendly relations with American imperialism. That tends unfortunately to be the character of the politics of these groups in this struggle.

At some point the situation could change in such a way that we would call for material support to the MPLA—or the UNITA, or the FNLA, or some combination of the three—while maintaining our political opposition to its program.

Our point of departure is opposition to American imperialist intervention, and if this ends up placing us in the same camp as one or another of the national liberation groups, then so be it.

It is possible that over time one or another of the three organizations could evolve in such a way that they would cease to be national liberation groups, would lose their mass support, would become puppets of imperialism. That could happen. At this stage there is no basic difference of this kind among the three groups.

Our opposition to the intervention of imperialism does not stem from any view that the imperialists are backing the wrong group or something like that. In our opinion, imperialism is intervening in this situation with the aim of imposing its control. Imperialism wants to hold back the independence of Angola, to weaken Angola in general. Even if we were to support the MPLA at some stage, we would not make the error of trying to pressure imperialism into supporting the MPLA.

I think it is important to note in addition that the American ruling class is not unanimous on the question of just which group to back. Even before the present debate there was pressure from those concerned about the danger of another Vietnam. The fact is that the American imperialist specialists in African affairs in the State Department were unanimously opposed to Kissinger's policy. They held that the United States should seek a diplomatic settlement between the three groups.

Richard Clark, the chairman of the Senate Foreign Relations Subcommittee on Africa, went to Angola and talked with the leaders in the MPLA. After he came back, he maintained that there was no basic difference among the three groups. He said that the MPLA leaders assured him that they would turn away from the Soviet Union as soon as they were able to beat the other groups.

I want to say a word about the campaign of the social democrats and the Maoists demanding that "the Russians" or "Soviet imperialism" get out of Angola. We are opposed to this.

There is no such thing as Soviet imperialism, anyway, and all this does is play into the hands of American imperialism. It equates Soviet aid to national liberation movements with attempts by the imperialists to maintain their economic exploitation and social oppression of the colonial countries.

As revolutionists and as unconditional supporters of the right to self-determination of the Angolan people, we of course criticize the Kremlin's inadequate aid to the struggle against imperialism. We criticize the Stalinists' uncritical support to MPLA policies, including the MPLA's chauvinist attitude toward the Bakongo and Ovimbundu peoples and its attempts to gain control over these peoples. We criticize the Kremlin's political course blocking the development of a revolutionary socialist party in Angola. We do not agree with the Stalinist policy.

The interests of the Angolan workers and peasants do not guide the Soviet bureaucracy, any more than the Soviet bureaucracy's policies represent the interests of the Soviet workers and peasants. But the threat, the danger in Angola is *imperialist* intervention.

Our job is to demand that the U.S. government get out. If the Soviet Union stopped sending weapons to the MPLA, would that be a step forward for the Angolan revolution? No. It would embolden imperialism!

We do not demand that *any* of the national liberation groups in Angola give up the arms they have received from *any* source.

It is the political course that all three groups have followed, not the source of their arms, that is playing into the hands of world imperialism. And as Peter Seidman pointed out, the last thing we want to do is give Washington any cover for its own intervention anywhere. This is a particularly scandalous aspect of the Maoists' and social democrats' demand for the Soviet Union to get out. It is a capitulation to the pressure of American imperialism.

What do we think should be done in Angola? First of all, we call for the unity, in anti-imperialist action, of the three nationalist organizations or any other similar organizations that may exist in Angola. We call on them to unite against the various imperialist powers that have intervened.

When the Portuguese ruled there, we were for the nationalist organizations uniting in action to drive the Portuguese out of Angola instead of each one of them trying to maneuver in various ways with the Portuguese. We propose the same course in response to South Africa or any other imperialist power trying to get involved. At the same time our basic objective is to help the masses break from these organizations on a political level.

We don't have a neutral attitude toward the three groups in relation to the civil war. We are against the policies of each of them in the civil war; we are against their refusal to follow a united policy against imperialism.

Instead of launching a national campaign to unite the various organizations against South Africa, the MPLA advanced militarily against the UNITA and to a lesser extent against the FNLA.

It is difficult at this distance to assess all the ins and outs of the factional war between the three groups. But we have no difficulty in seeing what our main job is, as Fred and other speakers pointed out. This is to organize opposition to American imperialist intervention, not only in words but in deeds.

We will do that and to the extent that the national liberation groups in Angola are also consistent in their struggle to end all imperialist intervention we will find ourselves in the same camp.

But it would be an obstacle to make an incorrect assessment on the basis of a one-sided set of facts, so that we would find ourselves in the factional camp of one of these nationalist groups pitted against the others without adequate justification.

That would stand as an obstacle in our battle against imperialism, just as it has among the various groups in Portugal and around the world, who place support of one of the groups above the needs of the struggle against imperialism.

The main thing that we have to act on right now is not the polemic going on between the various groups or the polemic on this question in the Fourth International. The main decision this plenum must make to advance the interests of the Angolan peoples and the African revolution as well as the American revolution is to launch a campaign around Angola.

We have to make the Socialist Workers Party the organization that is doing the most to get the United States out of Angola, that is trying to get everybody working together on this question, that is trying to override the factionalism engendered by the supporters of one or another of three groups.

I think that we are going to find a very broad response to such a campaign in the Black communities. I think we are going to find a good reception in the labor movement, in the student movement—wherever the Indochina experience is remembered.

Hands Off Angola!

[The following statement was adopted January 3, 1976, by the National Committee of the Socialist Workers Party.]

Immediate action is needed to stop the Democrats and Republicans from plunging the United States into a new war. Picket lines, teach-ins, rallies, and marches are required to get the message to Washington: Stop the U.S. intervention in Angola—Hands off!

Working people in this country have nothing to gain and everything to lose by Ford's intervention in the civil war in Angola. They have no interest in seeing tens of millions of dollars spent on another war while funds for education, health, and housing are slashed. And they have no interest in seeing American troops sent to die in Angola, which can happen if Washington's intervention escalates.

Black Americans in particular want no part of Ford's war policy. The American government has waged an unceasing war on the Black freedom struggle—in Africa and in the United States. Black Americans know better than anyone that Washington's policies are thoroughly racist. Why should they believe Ford's rhetoric about defending democracy in Africa, when they see the U.S. government refusing to enforce its own laws on desegregation at home?

Why should they believe that the CIA is fighting for freedom in Angola, when they know that the United States plotted to murder Patrice Lumumba, the Congolese rebel leader, just as it has conspired to disrupt and destroy the Black liberation movement in this country?

153

Why should they support the spending of millions of dollars for war in Angola, while social services desperately needed by the Black communities are being slashed?

The Ford administration has offered repeated assurances to the American people that the U.S. intervention in Angola is "not analogous" to the war in Vietnam. But Ford's policies point precisely to another Vietnam. Ford is involving the United States in a new colonial war, in which American financial resources and military might are committed to the protection of the profits and investments of the giant corporations.

For years the United States backed Portugal's colonial wars in Black Africa. Portuguese troops were trained in the United States, armed with U.S. weapons, and financed by U.S. dollars in their racist war to crush the African freedom fighters. Now, in the wake of the disintegration of Portugal's empire, Washington is moving toward direct intervention to impose its will on the peoples of Angola and to maintain imperialist control of that country.

This involvement runs the risk of escalation into a nuclear war that would destroy humanity.

As in Vietnam, Washington's moves have been carried out behind a screen of lies and secrecy. Despite the official denials, there ought to be no illusions about the U.S. aims in Angola. The war makers have been escalating their intervention step by step, testing the reaction, gauging how far they can go without generating a new antiwar movement.

Just as the anti-Vietnam War movement played a major part in forcing the United States to get out of Indochina, a movement against U.S. intervention in Angola can help prevent Washington from dragging the country into a new foreign adventure. The potential exists for such a movement to be built, and to win mass support.

The American people are already deeply distrustful of the government's aims and motives in Angola. The justifications offered by Ford and Kissinger for the U.S. operation in Angola are the same as those used in Vietnam: the need to "stop Communism" and to defend "national security" by intervening in a small country thousands of miles away.

Vietnam, Watergate, and the steady stream of disclosures about secret CIA plots abroad have left the American people with a healthy suspicion of government propaganda and deep opposition to any new imperialist adventures.

The hypocritical argument that Washington is acting to stop "Soviet colonialism" in Africa doesn't carry much weight with millions of people who are beginning to see that the real threat to the right of the peoples of the colonial world to self-determination comes from Washington.

Kissinger's claim that the goal is to defend self-determination is a transparent cover-up of the real U.S. role. Throughout southern Africa Washington has been a steadfast supporter of colonialism and apartheid.

United States backing of Portugal's colonial wars went hand in hand with its unwavering support to the white-settler regimes in South Africa and Rhodesia.

The deep and potentially explosive opposition to Ford's moves in Angola has already caused divisions within the U.S. ruling class over the tactical wisdom of Ford's policy. A section of this country's rulers believes that the danger of a political reaction against U.S. intervention, hand in hand with South Africa's apartheid regime, outweighs what could be gained through such a course. They argue that a new Vietnam could be disastrous for American imperialism.

It was the representatives of this point of view who carried the vote in the Senate on December 19 to cut off funds for "covert" operations in Angola.

But this Senate action, taken with much fanfare, isn't binding. Congress conveniently adjourned for the holidays before the measure could be taken up in the House, freeing Ford's hand for at least several more weeks of military aid and diplomatic maneuvering.

Just as happened time after time during the Vietnam War, the congressional war critics satisfied themselves with rhetoric about peace, while refusing to take action to get the United States out.

What an abdication of responsibility it would be for opponents of U.S. intervention in Angola to rely on the Democratic and Republican politicians to halt the U.S. war drive! The movement against the Vietnam War was successful because it did not trust the "doves" in Washington to live up to their peace promises. Instead, it mobilized millions of people in the streets.

The anti-Vietnam War movement learned that the only voice the "doves" ever responded to was the voice of masses of protesters.

The labor movement, the Black communities, the colleges and

high schools, ought now to become the arenas for antiwar discussion, education, and action.

All those who opposed the Vietnam War, and those who have marched against U.S. intervention in southern Africa, need to join forces in a determined effort to stop Ford's war plans in Angola.

The differing views that exist on the role and programs of the three liberation groups now involved in the civil war in Angola should not stand in the way of united actions by all supporters of the Angolans' right of self-determination.

Now is the time to launch a campaign of action to stop U.S. aggression and to let Washington know that the American people don't want another Vietnam. The Socialist Workers Party pledges its aid and support to build such a movement.

No secret war! Let the American people know the full truth about U.S. intervention!

Not one penny for war, not one soldier to Angola!

No more Vietnams! Hands off Angola!

Bibliography

Africa Research Group. *Race to Power: The Struggle for Southern Africa*. Garden City, New York: Doubleday, Anchor Press, 1974.

Birmingham, David. *The Portuguese Conquest of Angola*. London: Oxford University Press, 1965.

Chilcote, Ronald H. *Portuguese Africa*. Englewood Cliffs, New Jersey: Prentice-Hall, 1967.

Davidson, Basil. *In the Eye of the Storm*. Garden City, New York: Doubleday, 1972.

Duffy, James. *Portugal in Africa*. Baltimore: Penguin Books, 1962.

Institute of Race Relations. *Angola: A Symposium; Views of a Revolt*. London: Oxford University Press, 1962.

Instituto Superior de Ciências Sociais e Política Ultramarina. *Angola*. Lisbon: Universidade Tecnica de Lisboa, 1964.

The Kissinger Study on Southern Africa. Nottingham: Spokesman Books, 1975.

Marcum, John. *The Angolan Revolution*. Vol. 1: *The Anatomy of an Explosion (1950-1962)*. Cambridge: Massachusetts Institute of Technology Press, 1969.

Minter, William. *Portuguese Africa and the West*. Harmondsworth, Middlesex: Penguin Books, 1972.

Thompson, Leonard, and Butler, Jeffrey, eds. *Change in Contemporary South Africa*. Berkeley and Los Angeles: University of California Press, 1975.

Wheeler, Douglas L., and Pélissier, René. *Angola*. New York: Praeger Publishers, 1971.

Further Reading

For continuing news reports and analyses

INTERCONTINENTAL PRESS is an international Marxist newsweekly that specializes in political analysis and interpretation of events of particular interest to the labor, socialist, colonial independence, Black, and women's liberation movements.

Much of Ernest Harsch's material in *Angola: The Hidden History of Washington's War* was originally prepared for *Intercontinental Press* as part of its continuing coverage and analysis of the struggle in Angola. *IP* has also carried exclusive eyewitness reports by Tony Hodges from Angola.

Subscription rate: Six months—$12. One year—$24. Write for information about first class and airmail rates. Address: Intercontinental Press, P.O. Box 116, Village Station, New York, N.Y. 10014

THE MILITANT is a weekly socialist newspaper covering struggles against unemployment and inflation, racist discrimination, and the oppression of women, as well as international events. A unique source of news and analysis, the *Militant* has become the most widely read socialist newsweekly in the United States.

Subscription rates: Two months—$1. One year—$7.50. Address: The Militant, 14 Charles Lane, New York, N.Y. 10014

As Angola was winning its long struggle for independence from Portugal, the country was plunged into a civil war. Here is the documented record of the U.S. government's secret military intervention in Angola, in alliance with Portuguese colonialism and the racist regime of South Africa.

This book is also available in a clothbound edition at $9.

PATHFINDER PRESS
410 West Street, New York 10014 / 47 The Cut, London SE1 8LL

2053

DATE DUE

10 May 78			
GAYLORD			PRINTED IN U.S.A.